Resilient Code

Resilient Code
Maxims for Pain-free Programming

- S.O.L.I.D. foundations are long lived
- Interfaces are illustrations of needs not infrastructure
- When thou yields, thou knowest IEnumerable
- O(1) > O(N)
- Know thy tools
- Awaiting means not waiting
- No Test == No Proof
- Dependencies lacking injection are fixed anchors
- Tested anchors prove not boats float
- Empty assertions are blankets holding no heat
- new is a four-letter word
- Occam was right
- The most efficient function doesn't exist
- Too many ifs make for iffy code
- Do catch and throw. Do not catch and throw new
- The art of efficient code is NOT doing things
- The best refactors make extensive use of the delete key
- brvtbd
- Speed is a measurement of scale
- You cannot improve what you do not measure
- Your legacy is production code
- The only permanence is a lack thereof

Leonard Sperry

ISBN 9798774413713

Illustrations by Ed Scheer

First printing December 2021

https://github.com/leosperry/ResilientCode

Thank You

This book would not be possible without the many people that have helped me throughout my career. To Joe, who took a chance on a driver who went to night school and had no professional experience, thank you. To Nathan, who encouraged me to find new solutions and lead the technical direction for an entire product, thank you. To Kevin, Chad, and the other members of that team, thank you for the amazing teamwork which taught me the power of collaboration. To all the product owners, designers, and fellow engineers I've had the pleasure of working with throughout the years, thank you for all that you have done for and with me. To Katie, for helping me edit and teaching me some of the more nuanced grammar rules, thank you. Most of all, to my beautiful wife who has supported me every step in my career and encouraged me to write all these words, a big heart-felt thank you.

This book is dedicated to my mother Gay-Lynn aka Tweety
without whom my career would not have been possible.

Table of Contents

Preface...1
   How it all started...1
   About the Author...2
   About the Reader...3
   Format of the book and code.......................................3

SOLID foundations are long lived 5
   Single Responsibility Principle...............................5
   Open/Closed Principle 8
   Liskov Substitution Principle 10
   Interface Segregation Principle 13
   Dependency Inversion Principle.........................15

Interfaces are Illustrations of Needs, not Infrastructure 19

When thou yields, thou knowest IEnumerable 21
   Real world processing of large data sets 24
   The powers and pitfalls of System.Linq 32
   When is it appropriate to call *ToList*?............34

O(1) > O(N) 37
   Hidden Complexity...41

Know thy tools..45
   Integrated Development Environments (IDEs)....45
   Data Structures 46
   Alogorithms...46
   Libraries..46
   Frameworks...47
   Wait Statements..47

Awaiting means not waiting.....................................49
   ConfigureAwait(false)..52
   To async or not to async 53
   To Task or not to Task 54

No Test == No Proof...57
   The Testing Triangle..57
   Code Coverage 61

Dependencies Lacking Injection are Fixed Anchors.................63
   Arrange 65

Tested anchors prove not boats float **67**
    Act **67**

Empty assertions are blankets holding no heat....................................... **69**
    Assert **69**

new is a four-letter word **73**
    Inversion of Control Containers **75**

Occam was right... **79**
    Onion Architecture... **82**

The most efficient function doesn't exist **87**

Too many ifs make iffy code **91**

Do catch and throw. Do not catch and throw new. **95**
    Catching Exceptions **95**
    Throwing Exceptions **99**

The art of efficient code is NOT doing things **101**
    Access Modifiers **101**
    Patterns for sake of consistency over function **102**
    Fluent Syntax.. **105**

The best refactors make extensive use of the delete key...................... **109**

brvtybd **111**

Speed is a measurement of scale **113**
    Multi-threading... **114**
    Load Balancing and Message Queues... **121**
    Shallot Architecture **122**

You cannot improve what you do not measure **125**
    Performance Tests.. **125**
    Logs **126**
    Telemetry **129**
    Assembly Scanning... **130**

Your legacy is production code... **133**

The only permanence is a lack thereof **135**

What's not on the list? **137**

Reflection do's and don'ts **139**

Code Reviews **149**

Partnership *151*

Exit Code 0 .... *153*

References *155*

Index *157*

Preface

Over the course of my career as a software engineer, I have learned some extremely helpful principles that I have been able to boil down to little snippets. When I am trying to solve whatever today's problem is, I have been able to reach for them for guidance. When I am coaching a junior developer, they have been helpful to quickly explain how a larger abstract idea applies to a specific problem. They are not strict rules. They are maxims. The Merriam-Webster dictionary defines a maxim as "a general truth, fundamental principle, or rule of conduct." Oxford defines it as "A short, pithy statement expressing a general truth or rule of conduct." They are simple statements representing larger ideas intended to make you think about how to write code.

How it all started

Early in my career , I wrote a short list of some high-level concepts I wanted to focus on. About once a month, I would pull out the list and see how it was working for me. Over time, I added and removed ideas. After a few iterations, I noticed the list was starting to change less, and I started thinking of them like rules. I wanted a name for them. I'm a huge fan of Star Trek; there's an episode of *Star Trek: The Next Generation* called "The Game" where a character has a list of rules used to guide them throughout life. They were called "Robin's Laws." I thought maybe I would call them Leonard's Laws, but they weren't rules to my life. I also knew rules were meant to be broken and these were starting to feel like something more. They were like guideposts and something not entirely absolute. Perhaps they were bendable, but not breakable. I needed a different name.

After searching through several thesauri, I came across the word Tao. I learned that it translates to "path" and sometimes means the natural order of things. While everything in code is fabricated from someone's imagination, I've found that when you don't follow these "rules" or "guideposts," maintaining the codebase becomes more difficult and painful. But alas, I am not a follower or Taoism nor is humility one of my strong suits. Clearly a different word is needed.

I have called them adages, aphorisms, and guidelines. None of them quite felt right. Today, I simply call them my programming maxims. They are short, pithy, easy-to-remember statements to guide you in development. When you follow them, development feels much easier and more natural. The code becomes easier to maintain, modify, test, and so much more.

When I come across some witty sentence about code, I sometimes add it to my "Ideas Under Review." Over time, I shortened, combined, or replaced the snippets with something similar. If they stick around for a while, they get added to the list. The list will continue to change as our industry changes. For example, a decade ago, many, if not most, companies did not have rigorous unit testing standards. Now most companies do. These principles come from lessons I have learned. Sometimes, these lessons were painful. It's brutal trudging through a class in legacy code that is over 3,000 lines, desperately trying to keep track of non-obvious dependency graphs, and crossing your fingers that your one-line change won't have a disastrous down-stream effects. As you read through this book, you'll see examples of difficult code. It's easy to complain about difficult code. My goal is to show how thoughtful design can lessen these pains and help you to leave the code in a better state than when you started. This book is about those principles. Hopefully, you will find them as helpful to you as they have been to me.

So, why title the book *Resilient Code*? I went through literally hundreds of iterations before landing on "resilient." If you're like me, when you look back over your career and think about the most difficult challenges you've had developing software, it is not the applications you think about; it is the code. This book will not teach you how to write resilient applications with amazing fault tolerances and built-in redundancies. It will teach you how to write code that is easy to work with. When you deploy your application and the user finds some edge case you didn't consider, which users have an uncanny knack of doing, you will find it easier to assess and fix. The code is resilient because it is easy to adapt. It is flexible and pliable, not rigid and unyielding. You become more resilient in your ability to affect change. Ultimately, this book is about writing code with long-term sustainable value. It will be code less susceptible to future developers, yourself included, wanting to tear it all down and start over. The code itself will be more resilient and will stand the test of time.

About the Author

I grew up in the Pacific Northwest and have lived around the Puget Sound my entire life. As a child, I remember learning BASIC on a Commodore 64 and later I tinkered with its successor, the Amiga. I have always been fascinated with computers. Unfortunately, I did not fare so well in my adolescence and dropped out of high school. I took several jobs including waiter, shoe salesman, machine operator at a plastic injection molding factory, and courier. In my late twenties, I was working between six and seven days per week and up to 15 hours per day. I needed a change.

It was then that I heard advertisements on the radio for a non-accredited night school that taught networking and software. I chose the latter. There I learned HTML, CSS, and Java-Script, none of which existed in my youth. I learned about SQL and database normalization. Most of the coursework centered on C#. I learned how to use ASP.NET and web forms to connect it to HTML and how to use ADO.NET to connect it to SQL. I spent a year working a full-time job all day and spending every night and weekend either in school or studying. It was make-or-break for me. I never wanted to go back to 100-hour work weeks with no medical insurance. Going back to school was the best decision I had ever made for myself up to that point in my life.

My mother, who co-signed my school loan, died of liver cancer that year. It was both the hardest and best year of my life.

I tell you this because I want you to know how passionate I am about code. I'm not exaggerating when I say that C# saved my life. I have spent my career grateful for every opportunity and striving to hone my craft as a software engineer. My resume now says, "full stack generalist and .NET specialist." Today I work as a software architect for a fintech in Seattle.

About the Reader

The book is targeted to developers of all skill levels. I assume that you have a basic understanding of C#, the .NET framework, and automated testing. Many of the concepts in this book will carry over to other languages. Java developers will find many of the concepts helpful, but some of the book will focus on C# specific implementations. Previous exposure to Big-O notation will also be helpful.

This book holds a great deal for junior developers. I find that while college computer science programs teach you all the basics, seldom do new recruits know how to apply many principles in practice. A great example is recognizing when to use a *Dictionary* (hashset) instead of a *List*.

The book will help mid-level developers cement some of the fundamentals and encourage best practices more often. I find many mid-level engineers struggle with knowing when a rule is bendable vs breakable. This book will help in that regard.

Senior level developers will find some of the sections elementary. However, the maxims and the concepts they represent will help you in your mentoring efforts. Later chapters will look at the big picture and how to tie multiple applications together. Senior developers may find those chapters more engaging.

Format of the book and code

After starting with some foundational principles, we will dive into some low-level implementation specifics. We will then spend some time talking about automated testing, its importance, and how to get the most out of tests. Later, we'll take concepts already discussed and build upon them in how to create and structure applications. Eventually, we will talk about how to tie applications together and look at the big picture in terms of architecture.

I have already used words like "we" and "discuss." I want this book to feel very conversational. A former development manager of mine once told me that making great software is like making butter. When you make butter, you take heavy cream and beat it back and forth until you get butter. When two or more developers get together and beat the code back and forth, bouncing ideas off each other, eventually, you end up with the product you seek. Even though this book is a one-way conversation from me, the author, to you, the reader, I hope that I can anticipate your questions and provide good answers.

Class, property, method, and variable names, as well as C# keywords are *italicized*. When a word like "enumerator" is not italicized, it is talking about the concept or idea of an object, not the object used in programming. For example: The *User* model has properties describing the state of a user.

In code, I use underscores to prefix private variables. Some people with disagree with it, but I find it makes the code much easier to understand in terms of structure of the class and scope of the variables. When private member variables are not prefixed, it can often be hard to distinguish which variables are scoped to the class and which are scoped to the method. Having that understanding is critical to write thread-safe code.

Periodically, I will inject a note or tip into a chapter. When I do, I will call them out like this:

 Tip: This is an example of some additional information that will help you and/or pitfalls to watch out for

When you see them, they will be related to the subject being discussed, but not directly. Occasionally they will be a word of warning to avoid a pitfall. I have fallen into many in my career. Hopefully, I can save you the pain of climbing out.

SOLID foundations are long lived

SOLID is an acronym describing five design principles.

S: single responsibility principle
O: open/closed principle
L: Liskov substitution principle
I: interface segregation principle
D: dependency inversion principle

You may use some of these in your work every day, while hardly ever using others, but they are all exceptionally valuable. We often talk about code being tightly coupled as a bad thing. How do you define "tightly coupled"? Perhaps the easiest way to define tightly coupled code by what it is not: SOLID. There is a reason this maxim is first on the list. In fact, many of the other maxims on the list are related to one of the five SOLID principles in one way or another. Writing SOLID code decouples your application layers, which ultimately makes the code easier to maintain.

You have likely at least heard of many of the five principles and can talk to what they mean. I find many developers, however, struggle with identifying them in code or, more importantly, struggle to identify when an object's structure breaks one of the five principles. When you are digging through a mountain of interdependent legacy objects trying to find the source of a bug, knowing and identifying these principles can help you to locate the bug sooner and come up with a more robust solution.

You can find plenty of information about SOLID principles on the internet. Much of it is extremely technical and tells you how you should implement the principles. I have summarized their definitions to make them a bit more approachable.

My focus here is not so much on their technical details, but more about the idea of each and why they play a critical role. In this chapter, I will give examples for each of what happens when you break the principle and solutions on how to fix it.

Single Responsibility Principle

> *Every module, class, or function in a computer program should have responsibility over a single part of that program's functionality, which it should encapsulate.*

The single responsibility principle is the simple idea that each object should have a single responsibility. Sometimes it is easy to identify classes that break this principle. Introductory examples of Object-Oriented Programming (OOP) are full of them.

Let's take a common Car example. You have a *Car* class, a specialization, which derives from some *Automobile* class, an abstraction. You learn that objects have properties with getters and setters, that describe things like color, number of wheels, and size of engine. We learn about methods that can have overloaded polymorphic implementations such as drive, report speed, and open window. These are all great examples for learning OOP and what you can do with objects. Unfortunately, you don't always learn the difference between a car and a driver: A car is a thing, and a driver is an entity that takes actions like opening the window. The car doesn't open the window; the driver does.

This leads to classes that are blended models. Imagine a *User* class that has properties describing the attributes of the user. This class might be hydrated with data via the properties. It might have methods like *Message* that will send a message to the user. Already the class is beginning to take on multiple responsibilities.

In one instance I saw early in my career, a *User* class was used to do all of that and load information from a web form during user registration. Because a business rule said that a user must have a valid email, validation logic was used to validate the email in the setter of the *Email* property. Later, when the regular expression (often abbreviated regex) describing a valid email was changed, loading records from the database failed because the previously saved email didn't pass the new regex. This object clearly had too many responsibilities.

I used the term "blended model" above. Let's take a moment to talk about models. There are domain, data, and view models that all serve different purposes. You should only ever use any of them for transporting data, whether from the database, or from the view, or a business logic layer.

I have a collection of little starships at my desk, and I like to use them as an example. They are models, and they exist only to represent some real or imagined object, or state of an object. The moment you take a model and give it the ability to do something, it is no longer a model. A model car doesn't have an engine; a remote-controlled car does. Models should not do things. Objects like providers, services, and handlers should do things.

If your application is structured well, often you can use your domain models for data or view models as well, but if you need another model because the view needs things to look different, don't be afraid of making a new model for that single purpose. Make sure to not name them all the same thing, though.

I tend to use the domain model as much as possible since it represents the idea of what the object is best, but when I need a different model, I name it specifically. For example, I may have a *User* model that represents a user that interacts with the system. If I need a different model for sending information about the user to the database, I might name it *UserData-Model*.

Developers will sometimes get caught up on this idea. "What do you mean by Single Responsibility? Should every call to a database be wrapped into a single class?". It's a hard question to answer. Like many principles, it's easy to take it too far. So, how do you find the balance? There really is no right answer. You should be able to sum up the single responsibility in one short sentence, and the one sentence should avoid words like "every" or "all."

Let's take a look at some examples.

> *This object is responsible for retrieving all the billing information.*

You might have a class called *BillingProvider* and have good reason for that object, but what does that sentence mean? Does it retrieve invoices, billing addresses, line items, accounts, and the like?

You can see how that word "all" makes it easy to expand the scope. What if we said, "This object is responsible for sending all invoices to and from the database"?

That sounds much more reasonable, but still includes the "all." The difference is that you can remove the word "all" and no additional qualifiers are needed. If I ask, "Which billing information?" you could list off all the types of billing information. Conversely, if I ask, "Which invoices?" the answer will resemble something looking like a *where* clause.

Let's take a look at another example.

> *This object is responsible for saving information about a user when that information includes additional meta-data.*

This time the sentence is too specific. It has an additional clause at the end that nearly doubles the length of the sentence and sounds like a *where* clause.

One of the maxims on my "Items Under Review" list is "SRP is a two-way street." By this I mean that each object has a single responsibility, but it also means that each use case has an object which is singularly responsible.

For example, imagine you work for the Acme Widget Company. The product owner comes to you and tells you that the Wonder Widget has a new amazing property which needs to be represented everywhere the Wonder Widget is displayed on the website. There are a dozen places that need to be updated. You may have to update all the places in the user interface. Now imagine each of those dozen places also had their own way of retrieving a Wonder Widget from the database. Your work just doubled. Having a single provider for retrieving Wonder Widgets simplifies the code and makes it easier to maintain.

Open/Closed Principle

Software entities should be open for extension,
but closed for modification.

In C#, the most obvious infraction of the open/closed principle is seen when a developer uses the *new* keyword to override a method or property. In my entire career, I have never seen a use case where that was the right tool. Numerous modifiers in C# allow the right kinds of access to an object. If a method or property does not use either the *virtual* or *abstract* key words, likely it was never intended to be changed, and the author of the class never made that decision. You should not make that decision for the class you are inheriting from unless you understand all the implications. If you do understand the implications, you should add the *virtual* keyword to the parent. When the *new* keyword is used in that fashion, it breaks through where an object was correctly closed for modification and modifies it anyway.

What do classes look like when they are incorrectly open for modification?

Let's say you have an *InvoiceService* class, and it depends on several objects for working with invoices. One of those objects is a *LineItemValidator*. There are many types of line items that may appear on an invoice such as physical products, supplies used, services rendered, or taxes. Maybe we have a new type of line item and the existing *LineItemValidator* cannot sufficiently handle the new use case. So, we add a property to the *InvoiceServcie* for setting the validator, build a new type of *LineItemValidator,* and assign it to a property on the *InvoiceService*. The problem lies in the fact that we allowed the consumer to change the validator being used. Because a consumer can change the behavior of the *InvoiceService* by redefining one of its dependencies, it is open for modification.

A better approach is to address the shortcomings of the original validator. In this scenario, chances are that the *LineItemValidator* was closed for extension where it should be open. Remember it was not able to handle the new type of line item. If it were open for extension, we could extend its functionality to handle the new line-item type. Often, you can identify the code that is not open for extension by the existence of *switch* statements. Take a look at this implementation with some fictional business rules applied.

```
 1  class LineItemValidator
 2  {
 3    public bool IsValid(LineItem lineItem)
 4    {
 5      switch (lineItem.LineItemType)
 6      {
 7        case LineItemType.Product:
 8          return ValidateProduct(lineItem);
 9        case LineItemType.Service:
10          return ValidateService(lineItem);
11        case LineItemType.Tax:
12          return ValidateTax(lineItem);
13        default:
14          throw new Exception("unrecognized type");
15      }
16    }
17
18    private bool ValidateTax(LineItem lineItem)
19    {
20      return lineItem.Discount == 0;
21    }
22
23    private bool ValidateService(LineItem lineItem)
24    {
25      return lineItem.Description != null;
26    }
27
28    private bool ValidateProduct(LineItem lineItem)
29    {
30      return lineItem.Amount >= 0;
31    }
32  }
```

Here you can see that the validator is closed for extension. In order to pass in a new type of line-item, you must modify this code to accept the new line-item type. I am extremely cautious when and where I will use an *enum*. Too many times, I've seen them lead to code like this.

When you are thinking about using an *enum*, think twice. To help you decide if you should use an *enum* ask yourself this question, "Do I ever expect new values to be added to the *enum* over time?" If the answer is "no, never" an *enum* could be the right choice. If not, you may consider if you can solve the problem by other means. Have you considered generics? Does your *enum* represent a larger idea that may need a different abstraction?

You might even argue that this class is breaking the single responsibility principle. It is trying to validate every possible line item. Instead, it could hold onto a collection of rules and apply them all.

```
1  class ExtendableLineItemValidator
2  {
3      List<Func<LineItem, bool>> _validations =
4          new List<Func<LineItem, bool>>();
5
6      void AddValidation(Func<LineItem, bool> validation)
7      {
8          _validations.Add(validation);
9      }
10
11     bool Validate(LineItem lineItem)
12     {
13         return _validations.All(v => v(lineItem));
14     }
15 }
```

With this approach, when a new type of line-item is created, there is no need to change the validator itself. It is open for extension.

Liskov Substitution Principle

Objects should be able to be replaced with sub-types without changing the correctness of the application.

Don't use *abstract* classes. Enough said, moving on.

I'm kidding! Seriously, though, as I've gone through my career, I've used *abstract* classes less and less. Abstract classes are harder to unit test and require creating a test implementation because you cannot instantiate an *abstract* class.

Many times, you will see long inheritance chains when a developer chooses abstract classes. By the time you get down to the concrete implementation, even if that implementation is only a hundred lines long, the actual definition of the class might be several thousand lines long because of all its parents. That starts sounding like it's breaking the single responsibility principle.

That all being said, the Liskov substitution principle is all about inheritance. In some ways, it is an extension of the open/closed principle. Inheritance is a tool that is sometimes helpful. Let's make sure we get it right.

Before we do, let's take a moment to talk about thread safety. Classes are thread safe when multiple threads can interact with the class and not cause unintended consequences. In other words, no thread can leave the object in a state that would cause work on another thread to be invalid.

I can't tell you the number of times I've seen *abstract* classes that were not built with thread safety in mind. They are easy to spot. The class will have some *private* or *protected* member, usually a collection, created or modified in one method. Later, some other method reads from that collection. Usually, one or both of those methods will be *abstract* or *virtual*.

There is a name for this anti-pattern: **temporal coupling**. Temporal coupling occurs when a developer structures a class so that it requires the consumer to call methods in a certain order. Some objects like a *Queue* inherently work because first someone queues an item, then later the objects are dequeued. The order of the calls is important. Data structures tend to rely on methods being called in a certain order. They help manage state.

However, generally speaking, temporal coupling is a bad practice. This anti-pattern is usually not thread safe. In our example where a shared collection is created, then read, if a second thread calls the first method before the first thread has a chance to call the second method, the collection is not correct. Worse, it could lead to non-performant code with additional locks to attempt thread safety.

Most of the time, the original developer intended the class to be newly constructed every time it was needed. This can become an issue when legacy code is modernized to use Inversion of Control (IOC) containers where it is easy to create singletons to save memory and processing.

Here's an example of such a class with temporal coupling.

```
 1  abstract class SomeBusinessServiceBase
 2  {
 3      private List<SomeBusinessObject> _objects;
 4
 5      protected abstract void LoadData();
 6
 7      public virtual void Render()
 8      {
 9          foreach (var item in _objects)
10          {
11              Console.WriteLine(item);
12          }
13      }
14  }
```

So, how does this all relate to Liskov? Imagine one implementation of this abstract class was modified so that when the collection is set, it is also sorted, and the second method that reads the collection relies on the collection being sorted. Now imagine a second implementation of the *abstract* class is built where the developer is not aware of the dependency of the collection being sorted. When they implement the first method and don't sort it, it breaks the second. This is where Liskov comes into play. In this example, when the original implementation is substituted for the new one, it breaks the correctness of the application.

Fortunately, fixing this scenario is straightforward. Let's take a look at how to fix it.

First, fix the temporal coupling. To do that, have the first method return the collection and have the second take it in as a parameter. That also fixes the thread safety issues. Now the collection can't be modified by another thread.

```
 1  abstract class SomeBusinessServiceBaseFixed
 2  {
 3      protected abstract IEnumerable<SomeBusinessObject> GetData();
 4
 5      public virtual void Render(IEnumerable<SomeBusinessObject> objects)
 6      {
 7          foreach (var item in objects)
 8          {
 9              Console.WriteLine(item);
10          }
11      }
12  }
```

Second, to adhere to Liskov, move the sorting logic to the second method. If it relies on the collection being sorted, have it sort the collection. Perhaps, after the bug is fixed, you revisit these classes' structure entirely. Should you never use an abstract class? While I'm not going to ban a specific coding practice, I will say that by avoiding abstract classes where possible, you also avoid all the pitfalls associated with the Liskov substitution principle and make the concrete implementations less complex.

Interface Segregation Principle

Many smaller interfaces are better than one large interface.

In the previous section, I said to avoid *abstract* classes, but what about an *interface*? Absolutely yes. Use interfaces and use many of them.

Interfaces are like contracts. When you look at implementing a new feature that requires changes up the entire stack, a team can develop a handful of interfaces quickly that allow them to each work in a different part of the stack and not rely on some concrete implementation to be complete in order for them to test their code.

Interfaces make unit testing a breeze because mocking frameworks, which work better with interfaces than abstrat classes, allow us to test our classes without relying on implementations.

I've heard many times that when you make interfaces for everything, it doubles the amount of code you need to define your application. To that I would say: First, that extra work pays off amply.

Second, it's true that you don't need interfaces for everything. A plain old CLR object (POCO) model with only properties does not need an interface. An *internal* helper or utility class may not need an interface. However, anywhere you cross an application boundary, do make sure to use interfaces. For example, use an interface when the business logic talks to the data layer, or the hosting application talks to the business services.

More specifically, the interface segregation principle makes it so that consumers do not have a reference to, or become encumbered by, methods they don't use.

Let's take a look at an example. For this example, we're going to use a *MessageBus* class. It will be responsible for consuming messages and passing them on to subscribers. Different consumers of the class have differing needs. Some need to receive messages, and others need to send messages. A publisher will only rarely need to also subscribe, and even if they do, they will likely be subscribing to a different topic or queue. The consumer should take a dependency only on the methods it needs. Instead of taking a dependency on an *IMessageBus*, a class needing to publish should take a dependency on a more specific *IPublisher* interface, and a subscriber should take a dependency on an *ISubscriber* interface. You may indeed have an *IMessageBus*. However, it would implement both the *IPublisher* and *ISubscriber* interfaces.

```
1  public interface IMessageBus
2      : IPublisher, ISubscriber
3  {}
4
5  public interface IPublisher
6  {
7     void Publish(object message);
8  }
9
10 public interface ISubscriber
11 {
12    void Subscribe(string topic, Action<object> messageHandler);
13 }
```

It's unusual to see a bug caused by breaking the Interface Segregation Principle, but following it can make refactoring code much easier later.

Dependency Inversion Principle

When following this principle, the conventional dependency relationships established from high-level, policy-setting modules to low-level, dependency modules are reversed.

Of the five SOLID principles, this is perhaps the singularly most important, and the hardest to get used to.

Most of the time, when you talk about the dependency inversion principle, you'll also be talking about inversion of control (IOC) and dependency injection (DI). There are at least a dozen commonly used IOC containers available to .NET developers, and I highly recommend using one in all your applications. While evaluating features of differing IOC containers are beyond the scope of this book, any of the popular options will serve nearly, if not, all your needs. In a later chapter, we will talk about how to use an IOC container.

We are going to focus on dependency inversion and dependency injection here.

So, what is the difference between dependency inversion and dependency injection? Simply, dependency inversion looks at the way classes are related to each other. Dependency injection is means by which we accomplish dependency inversion.

Before we get to using DI, let's talk about what it looks like when you don't have it. Often, you'll have some business service that needs to get access to some data store. You might see in these business logic classes that when there is a need for data access, they either call the constructor for a data access object or call a static method on the data access class to get an instance of the data access layer (DAL). In either case, the business service is dependent on the specific implementation of the DAL, and it must know about the construction method at the time it is needed. If there is a change in the way the DAL is constructed, all the classes that call the construction method must be modified, and those changes happen more often than you might think.

Here is a brief example.

```
 1  public class SomeBusinessService
 2  {
 3      public IEnumerable<SomeBusinessObject>
 4          GetObjectsForSpecialUseCase(int categoryId)
 5      {
 6          DataAccessLayer dal = new DataAccessLayer();
 7          var objects = dal.GetObectsFiltered(categoryId);
 8          foreach (var item in objects)
 9          {
10              //perform some domain logic
11          }
12          return objects;
13      }
14  }
```

You can see on line 6 that the constructor for the DAL is called. Unfortunately, most constructors are not empty constructors. Imagine the DAL has a dependency on a logger that is passed into the constructor.

What if at some point we want to change to use a different logger? Perhaps someone discovers a security flaw in the logger we were using and your information security department requires all implementations of that logger to be replaced as soon as possible. If your data access layer now needs a new logger passed to it, all the business services must now also know how to construct the logger. That may trickle up the application to all the places in the hosting application where the business services are called.

A better approach is to inject the dependency and invert it. This way the business service does not need to know anything about how to construct a logger.

You can achieve dependency inversion via injection multiple ways: property injection, method injection, and constructor injection. Each has their place.

Property injection is where the class has a property that can be set. It can be helpful when you want to have some default behavior which a consumer can override should you choose.

Method injection is where the consumer tells your implementation at the time a method is called which version of the dependency should be used.

Constructor injection will be your go-to method. When combined with an IOC container, it entirely removes the responsibility of deciding how to construct an object at method execution and moves that logic to start up routines. When following this pattern, objects are designed specifically to not know about the implementations of other classes. The benefits of this approach are numerous, several of which we will discuss in detail in later chapters.

Here is an example of the same code above using constructor injection with some logging added into the business layer.

```
1  public class BusinessServiceWithDependencyInversion
2      : IBusinessServiceWithDependencyInversion
3  {
4      readonly IObjectProvider _objectProvider;
5      readonly ILogger _logger;
6
7      public BusinessServiceWithDependencyInversion(
8          IObjectProvider objProvider, ILogger logger)
9      {
10         _objectProvider = objProvider;
11         _logger = logger;
12     }
13
14     public IEnumerable<SomeBusinessObject>
15         GetObjectsForSpecialUseCase(int categoryId)
16     {
17         _logger.Log("beginning complex domain logic");
18         var objects = _objectProvider.GetObjectsByCategory(categoryId);
19         foreach (var item in objects)
20         {
21             //perform some domain logic
22         }
23         _logger.Log("completed complex domain logic");
24         return objects;
25     }
26 }
```

In the example above, you can see there is no dependency on any concrete data access layer or logger. Either implementation could be changed and there would be no need to change this business service. Additionally, you can see that this service implements an interface. That means the consumers of this service need not know about any implementation details inside this class.

By using interfaces as your dependencies, you make clearer lines of separation. If you have a dependency on a concrete class, you must have a reference to it. That means you must have a reference to the library in which it resides and all the dependencies it has.

Interfaces, when done well, rarely refer to classes outside of what is built into .NET. This makes it even easier to deploy changes and manage changes on an even larger scale.

Following the dependency inversion principle with extensive use of interfaces as a matter of habit will benefit your organization for years to come.

Interfaces are Illustrations of Needs, not Infrastructure

In the last chapter, we discussed how helpful interfaces can be. In this chapter, we explore when to use interfaces and how to write them.

You probably recall that simple plain old CLR objects (I'll call them POCOs from here on out) don't need interfaces. I also mentioned that *internal* helper objects might not need them. So, when should you write them? I write them:

- Anywhere I cross an application boundary.
- Any time I have a class with domain specific methods.

Understanding what I mean by "my domain" is a critical distinction. Is it in my domain to understand an HTTP call? As a developer, yes. As person trying to accomplish some business need, no. Interfaces should describe some business need.

Let's build on the example from the last chapter where a business service had a dependency on some data access. In this case we need to write a file. You may have an interface that looks something like this:

```
1 public interface IFileWriterBad
2 {
3     void Initialize(char driveLetter, string path);
4     bool WriteFile(Stream s);
5 }
```

Now we have an interface that our domain logic can use when it needs to write a file. If that business logic is structured well, the reference to this *IFileWriter* will be injected. This means that we can easily test the domain logic without writing an actual file.

There are two problems with this interface, both of which appear on line 3.

The first issue is that there are references to a specific technology—in this case, a local hard drive. Perhaps we have technical requirements due to constraints on the system, but technology requirements are not domain or business requirements. All the business really cares about is that the file was saved. How and where the file is saved is of little consequence.

The second issue is that the initialize method is a part of the interface. Again, this is not a business need. Your product owner is never going to come to you with a requirement to initialize your data access layer.

Why is this a problem? Imagine your product owner comes to you and says, "Now that we've moved this application to the cloud, we'd like to take advantage of managed cloud services for file storage, which will save us thousands of dollars annually in hardware." The managed service knows nothing about drive letters. It lives in the cloud where all drives are virtualized. While we've successfully designed unit testable code with clearly defined layers and small responsibilities, we've still taken a dependency on implementation details. In order to move to the managed service, you'll have to update all of the classes that consume the *IFileWriter* interface.

Let's take a look at a better solution: Leaving the implementation details to the class that implements the interface, as shown here:

```
1  public interface IFileWriter
2  {
3     bool WriteFile(Stream s);
4  }
5
6  public class FileWriter : IFileWriter
7  {
8     public FileWriter(char driveLetter, string path)
9     {
10       /* initialization logic and infrastructure dependent references
11        * belong to the class not the interface */
12    }
13
14    public bool WriteFile(Stream s)
15    {
16       throw new NotImplementedException();
17    }
18 }
```

Now when we want to change storage providers, changing the code becomes a breeze. To move to the new cloud provider, we will have to implement a new version of the *IFileWriter* — work we'll have to do regardless of implementation. However, with this updated interface, we will no longer need to change all the consumers of the interface. If an IOC container is used, switching to the new implementation is likely a one-line change to our application's startup routines.

By not including technology or infrastructure specific references in our interfaces, our code becomes more adaptable and resilient.

When thou yields, thou knowest IEnumerable

The *yield return* statement is potentially one of the most powerful and useful in C#, yet few developers know when to use it or how to use it effectively, perhaps because few other languages have a functional equivalent. *Yield return* allows us to abstract the idea of iterating over a series without taking a dependency on any specific data structure.

Before we jump into how a *yield return* allows you to return an *IEnumerable* without instantiating it, let's take a deeper dive into what *IEnumerable* actually is.

The *IEnumerable* interface has a single-method *GetEnumerator,* which returns an *IEnumerator*. The enumerator accesses a series of objects sequentially, most often, although not exclusively, to iterate over a collection.

Let's take a look at an example.

```
 1 public interface IEnumerable
 2 {
 3     IEnumerator GetEnumerator();
 4 }
 5
 6 public interface IEnumerator
 7 {
 8     object Current { get; }
 9     bool MoveNext();
10     void Reset();
11 }
```

Most of the time you don't need to worry about how to use *IEnumerable*. You do need to know how a *foreach* statement uses *IEnumerable* every time you use a *foreach*. Let's take a look at two functionally equivalent snippets to see how this works.

```
 1 public void ForeachIteration(IEnumerable enumerable)
 2 {
 3    foreach (var item in enumerable)
 4    {
 5       // do work
 6    }
 7 }
 8
 9 public void WhileIteration(IEnumerable enumerable)
10 {
11    var enumerator = enumerable.GetEnumerator();
12    while (enumerator.MoveNext())
13    {
14       var item = enumerator.Current;
15       // do work
16    }
17    enumerator.Reset();
18 }
```

You can see that the enumerator does all the heavy lifting by keeping track of the state. Also notice the *Reset* method. You may have seen error messages indicating that you cannot modify a collection while it is being iterated. This is because the enumerator is managing the state. Modifying the collection invalidates that state.

Now let's look at the *yield return* statement. In this example, we are returning a series without ever instantiating a collection.

```
 1 public IEnumerable<int> PrimeNumbersLessThan10()
 2 {
 3    yield return 1;
 4    yield return 2;
 5    yield return 3;
 6    yield return 5;
 7    yield return 7;
 8 }
```

There are two awesome things about a *yield return* statement: First, it allows you to defer execution. In between all the calls to *yield,* you can add any logic you like and defer the execution of that code until the moment it is needed. When the *PrimeNumbersLessThan10* method is called, it doesn't actually return the series. It does return a reference to an *IEnu-*

merable. When the *IEnumerable* is iterated, it calls the *GetEnumerator* method similar to the way our *while* loop used it. Internally, that enumerator keeps track of what has been executed and what hasn't.

Second, and more importantly, it allows you to move through a series without allocating the entire series to memory. In this example, there is no *List* or array. It is simply a well-structured call stack that gives you the items as you need them.

Like magic, when the *yield return* statement is compiled, it returns a reference to an *IEnumerable* with an enumerator that calls back into your method. The enumerator that gets created might look something like this:

```
1  class MagicEnumerator : IEnumerator
2  {
3      private Func<IEnumerable> _collectionGetter;
4
5      public object Current { get; private set; }
6
7      public MagicEnumerator(Func<IEnumerable> collectionGetter)
8      {
9          _collectionGetter = collectionGetter;
10     }
11
12     public bool MoveNext()
13     {
14         var hasMoreItems = GetOne(out var item);
15         if (hasMoreItems)
16         {
17             Current = item;
18         }
19         return hasMoreItems;
20     }
21
22     public void Reset()
23     {
24         // compiler magic that resets the state of the _collectionGetter
25     }
26
```

```
27  private bool GetOne(out object item)
28  {
29      bool ranToCompletion = false;
30      /*
31       * Compiler magic that knows how to call the underlying reference
32       * to the _collectionGetter and returns a single item
33       *
34       * if the _collectionGetter has run to completion
35       * sets ranToCompletion to true
36       */
37      item = default;
38      return !ranToCompletion;
39  }
40 }
```

 Line 37 would not actually set *item* to *default*. It would get a single item from *_collectionGetter*. The important thing is that the enumerator knows how to return a single item and that the method returning the *IEnumerable* has completed.

Here we see some compiler magic, but how can we use that to make our code magic? Imagine you are working with an extremely large data set. In one case I've seen, the business was processing CSV files that were multiple gigabytes in size. We weren't generating them, but we were consuming them from another company. Your data set could just as easily be a database table. The point is, that if your application tries to load that entire data set into memory, you will soon find yourself running into an *OutOfMemoryException*.

Real world processing of large data sets

Many times, developers look to batching when confronted with a situation like this. While batching can solve the problem, it is often not the most efficient. Let's look at the CSV example with a simple console application, but instead of batching, we'll stream all the records to the database using a *yield return*.

```
 1 private static void Main(string[] args)
 2 {
 3    StreamReader rdr = new StreamReader("path to file");
 4    string line;
 5    int lineCount = 0;
 6    while ((line = rdr.ReadLine()) != null)
 7    {
 8       //process the line
 9       lineCount++;
10    }
11    Console.WriteLine($"{lineCount} lines processed");
12 }
```

With the approach shown in the example, we can process the entire file while only allocating one line to memory at a time.

What if processing that line requires complex business logic, and after we process it, we need to save the results? I shouldn't put all that logic inside the while loop. That would break the single responsibility principle. Even if we did, how would we unit test our business logic without relying on a physical data store or file? After I process it, how do I save it to disk without loading the entire data set into memory? That's where the *yield return* statement is our friend.

Let's expand this example to something a little more realistic. Imagine that a product owner gives us this set of requirements:

- We must process a file that has been delivered to our FTP server daily.
- The size of the file can range from several kilobytes to several gigabytes.
- The file is a CSV with the following columns:
  - account name (string)
  - account id (integer)
  - value (decimal)
- If the name is longer than 50 characters, we should truncate it. If it is empty, we should skip the record.
- If the account id is a negative number or we are unable to parse it, we should skip the record.
- If the value is empty or we are unable to parse it, we should skip the record.
- Inability to process any record should not cause the entire process to fail.
- All records should be stored to the account table in the database.

Given the above requirements, we can already begin to identify certain layers of the application. We need a layer to read the CSV, another to process the business rules surrounding how we handle invalid data, and another to save what we can process to the database. The console application will house all these objects and coordinate communication between them.

Before we get to any implementation, let's take what we learned from the last chapter and create some interfaces based on the business rules our product owner gave us.

```
1 interface ICsvReader<T> where T: class
2 {
3     IEnumerable<T> Read();
4 }
5
6 interface IAccountParsingLogic
7 {
8     string GetNameForSaving(string input);
9     int? GetAccountNumber(string input);
10    decimal? GetValue(string input);
11    bool AccountIsValid(Account account);
12 }
13
14 interface IAccountProvider
15 {
16    void SaveAccounts(IEnumerable<Account> accounts);
17 }
```

Now that we have some interfaces defined, we could have four developers begin work at the same time, One on each interface, and one to build the application coordinating their interaction. Each developer could test their layer independently of the others to ensure each part of the application functions correctly.

We'll take the interfaces one by one, starting with the CSV reader.

```
1  class CsvReader<T> : ICsvReader<T> where T : class
2  {
3     string _path;
4     Func<string[], T> _lineParser;
5     public bool FileHasHeader { get; set; } = true;
6
7     public CsvReader(string path, Func<string[], T> lineParser)
8     {
9        _path = path;
10       _lineParser = lineParser;
11    }
12
13    public IEnumerable<T> Read()
14    {
15       StreamReader rdr = new StreamReader(_path);
16       if (FileHasHeader)
17       {
18          //ignore the first line
19          rdr.ReadLine();
20       }
21       string line;
22       T item;
23       while ((line = rdr.ReadLine()) != null)
24       {
25          item = null;
26          try
27          {
28             item = _lineParser(line.Split(','));
29          }
30          catch (Exception)
31          {
32             //handle the exception
33          }
34          if (item != null)
35          {
36             yield return item;
37          }
38       }
39    }
40 }
```

Here we've created a generic version of a CSV reader that can be reused for other object types. The reading of the line has nothing to do with turning that line into a business object. That is a dependency we injected into the constructor via the *lineParser*. If there is a problem parsing any individual line, the line is skipped and processing continues. Critically, line 36 has our *yield return* statement. The logic will be executed only when the *IEnumerable* returned by the *Read* method is iterated. This ensures that we never load more than a single line of the file into memory. With this approach, we could handle a file of any size, even a petabyte!

 Note: We can make it better. If we need functionality to optionally stop processing on an error, we could add another property similar to the *FileHasHeader* property. This simple parser also does not handle quoted values or values with a comma in them. You can find CSV readers available that will do all that for you and more. The point of this exercise is to demonstrate the *yield return*. If this were production code, you'd want to take care to handle those use cases.

The implementation for the account parsing logic will be pretty straightforward. Let's take a look:

```
1 class AccountParsingLogic : IAccountParsingLogic
2 {
3     public bool AccountIsValid(Account account)
4     {
5         return
6             account.ID > 0 &&
7             !string.IsNullOrEmpty(account.Name) &&
8             account.Value != null;
9     }
10
11    public int? GetAccountNumber(string input)
12    {
13        if (int.TryParse(input, out int accountNumber))
14        {
15            return accountNumber;
16        }
17        return null;
18    }
19
```

```
20    public string GetNameForSaving(string input)
21    {
22        if (string.IsNullOrEmpty(input))
23        {
24            return null;
25        }
26        return input.Length > 50 ? input.Substring(0, 50) : input;
27    }
28
29    public decimal? GetValue(string input)
30    {
31        if (decimal.TryParse(input, out decimal val))
32        {
33            return val;
34        }
35        return null;
36    }
37 }
```

There is nothing fancy in this class, and different people have different styles for how to perform validation logic. The important thing to remember is that we separated the domain logic into its own layer, and none of this logic is inside a giant *foreach* loop.

The account provider is also straightforward:

```
 1 class AccountProvider : IAccountProvider
 2 {
 3     public void SaveAccounts(IEnumerable<Account> accounts)
 4     {
 5         foreach (var account in accounts)
 6         {
 7             // save to the database
 8         }
 9     }
10 }
```

I didn't flesh out the actual call to the database here because you can find libraries to help you do that. The thing to remember here is that there is a *foreach* loop. No other layer has seen that so far. This is where the enumerator from our method in the CSV reader will actually be called. This implementation would create a connection to the database for each record, but using what you learn in this chapter, you can come up with strategies to stream the results to the database.

 Bonus Challenge:
The *System.Data.SqlClient.SqlBulkCopy* class has an overload that takes in an *IDataReader*. You can create your own implementation of that interface that takes in an *IEnumerable<T>*. If you pass your collection to the *SqlBulkCopy* class via your own *IDataReader*, you can stream your results to the database in a single SQL command. Other frameworks or databases may also offer you ways of streaming input for serialization.

Now that we've written all the layers, let's wire them up and see it in action.

```
1  static void Main(string[] args)
2  {
3      AccountParsingLogic logic = new AccountParsingLogic();
4
5      Func<string[], Account> lineParser = cells => {
6          var id = logic.GetAccountNumber(cells[0]);
7          var name = logic.GetNameForSaving(cells[1]);
8          var value = logic.GetValue(cells[2]);
9
10         if (id.HasValue)
11         {
12             return new Account()
13             {
14                 ID = id.Value,
15                 Name = name,
16                 Value = value
17             };
18         }
19         return null;
20     };
21
22     var csvReader = new CsvReader<Account>("path to file", lineParser);
23
24     var accounts = csvReader.Read().Where(acct => acct != null);
25
26     var accountProvider = new AccountProvider();
```

```
27    accountProvider.SaveAccounts(accounts);
28 }
```

We might take the parsing logic and move it to its own class. Asking, "What is the application layer responsible for?" We answer: The application layer is responsible for taking input and passing it to the domain logic. This code does that.

Take a moment to go through this and think about where the application layer executes the *lineParser* function. Even though we declared it on line 5 and passed it to the CSV reader on line 22, *lineParser* doesn't actually get executed until line 27. We only have one *foreach* statement, inside the *SaveAccounts* method. That is where the *GetEnumerator* method is called and our *yield return* statement in the *CsvReader* gets utilized.

You may have noticed the *System.Linq* call to *Where* on line 24. You might be thinking that will iterate the collection. It doesn't. That's what people mean when they say that Linq defers execution. Inside most of the Linq methods, they *yield return*. That's what makes them so powerful and helpful.

However, System.Linq does have some pitfalls, you should be aware of them in order to use it to its full potential.

The powers and pitfalls of System.Linq

Linq stands for Language Integrated Query. Inherently, it deals with collections — specifically *IEnumerable*. Most of its methods are built as extension methods to *IEnumerable*.

System.Linq is arguably in the top three additions to .NET, along with TPL and support for generic types. It is incredibly powerful in its simplicity. The old maxim, "with great power comes great responsibility" certainly applies to Linq. There are two ways to consume Linq. First, it offers a set of methods extending *IEnumerable,* including the following non-exhaustive list. I have taken liberty to group the methods into 4 categories.

Filters / Sorters	Selectors	Aggregators	Concretors
Where	Select	Any	ToArray
Distinct	SelectMany	All	ToList
Except	GroupBy	Contains	ToDictionary
Intersect	Join	Aggregate	ToHashSet
Take	Union	Average	ToLookup
Skip	Concat	Count	
OrderBy		First	
ThenBy		Last	
		ElementAt	

Everything in the **Filters/Sorters** and **Selectors** columns will defer execution. Let's dive into those for a moment before exploring the **Aggregators** and **Concretors** columns.

- **Filters/Sorters:** Methods that help you find the elements of a collection you are interested in and orders them. The methods extend *IEnumerable<T>* and return you the same *IEnumerable<T>* type.
- **Selectors:** Extend *IEnumerable<T>* and can return you a different *IEnumerable<T>*. They can be very useful for turning data models into domain models or domain models into view models.

Everything in the first two columns use the *yield return* statements. For example, let's take a closer look at the *Where* method and how it might be implemented.

```
 1  public static IEnumerable<T> Where<T>(this IEnumerable<T> collection,
 2      Func<T, bool> filter)
 3  {
 4      foreach (var item in collection)
 5      {
 6          if (filter(item))
 7          {
 8              yield return item;
 9          }
10      }
11  }
```

It really is that easy, and demonstrates how *Linq* defers execution. Any logic you add to the *filter* will be executed during the iteration, when or wherever that may be.

Everything in the **Aggregators** and **Concretors** columns iterate the enumerable.

- **Aggregators:** Extend *IEnumerable<T>* and return you a single value.
- **Concretors:** Return some concrete collection. They are incredibly useful and can be incredibly dangerous.

How are concretors dangerous? Back when Linq first came out, many people said, "Linq defers execution. So, to protect yourself from unintended consequences, you should always concrete the collection." Although there is some truth to that, it is also misleading, and less experienced developers may think, "OK, I should always call *ToList*."

If you find yourself constantly using *ToList*, I entreat you to reconsider that advice. Like many things in software development, Linq is a suite of tools. You must know when to use one particular tool or not. Have I ever used a hammer to drive a screw? Yes. Should I use a hammer to drive a screw? Probably not. *ToList* and its partner *ToArray* are hammers. Make sure to choose the right tool for the job.

For example, let's look back to the previous section where we were processing a CSV. Line 24 looked like this:

```
 1  var accounts = csvReader.Read().Where(acct => acct != null);
```

If we had called *ToList* at the end of that line, all the work we did to defer execution would be lost, and the entire gigabyte file would be loaded into memory bringing our application to its knees.

When is it appropriate to call *ToList*?

There is no easy answer to that question. Use *ToList* to protect the consumer from potential performance issues. Try not to use it as a consumer unless you know the code you are consuming has potential performance flaws. My best advice: Consider concreting the collection if your method is returning an *IEnumberable* and iterating it will cause a database connection or trigger complex logic, and you don't want the consumer to accidentally run it more than once. Avoid concreting the collection where the execution is nominal, as in the case above with the call to *Where*. Use *ToList* to protect the consumer from potential performance issues. Try not to use it as a consumer unless you know the code you are consuming has potential performance flaws.

Under my "Ideas Under Review," I have "Use of *System.Linq.Enumerable.Count* should be a compiler error." It is a bold statement—one reason I haven't officially added it to the list yet. But it's driven by this type of example, which I've seen too many times:

```
1  if (someCollection.Count() > 1)
2  {
3      foreach (var item in someCollection)
4      {
5          // do work
6      }
7  }
```

The call to *Count* iterates the collection, as does the *foreach,* causing it to be iterated twice when once will suffice. This can be easily fixed by calling *Any* instead of *Count*. Keep in mind that *Any* will still call the iterator, and if we think about our CSV example, it will grab a file handle to read the first line, but at least it won't iterate the entire file. I often also see *Count* used when you need a record count.

For example, you might see this in a Controller where the result will be serialized to JSON.

```
1  return new {
2      data = someCollection,
3      recordCount = someCollection.Count()
4  };
```

If the collection is small enough, the performance issues could be negligible—but you can't guarantee the collection's size. Although *Linq* is a powerful tool, it isn't always the right tool. If you need to transform a collection and get a record count from it, instead of writing two *Linq* statements that both iterate the collection, consider using a single *foreach* to do both operations in one iteration.

The actual implementation of *Count()* uses reflection to determine the concrete type of the *IEnumerable*. In the case that the *IEnumerable* is actually a *List, Array*, or one of the other types with a *Count* property, it will use the *Count* property instead of iterating the collection. *Linq* is trying to save you from a costly mistake. If your reference to a collection is of such a type, use the *Count* property instead of the *Count()* or *Any()* methods.

However, I have too many times heard the argument that the performance concerns of using *Count()*, because of the reflection call, are negligible. That *if* statement inside of *Count()* is a very big *if*. You cannot and should not rely on it, especially if your only reference is to an *IEnumerable*. The fact that reflection is being used to avoid a potentially costly operation should be scary enough for you to never use it.

The other way to use *Linq* is with query syntax. Although some developers have an aversion to it, I use both functional and query syntax, depending on the situation.

Consider this example: We want to get all the categories that are used in a collection of books. Both *books* and categories are collections, where *Book* and *Category* are POCO models.

```
1 var categoriesUsedInBooks =
2    from catId in books.SelectMany(b => b.CategoryIds).Distinct()
3    join cat in categories
4    on catId equals cat.ID
5    select cat;
```

Even though you could validly argue that this type of logic perhaps belongs in a database, there will be times you need to compare two different collections. Perhaps one of the collections came from the input of the application and the other comes from the database. The point is that the above query may be harder to understand when written out using functional syntax. Developers who have an aversion to this syntax would likely break the logic up to one or multiple *foreach* statements, but I find this syntax be much clearer and more concise.

Also, there are times that you can do things in query syntax that cannot be done in functional syntax, because all the variables you define in the query syntax stay in scope for the entire statement. With functional syntax, they only stay in scope for the specific function that is being called.

 Tip:
When using query syntax, take advantage of the *let* keyword.

This chapter started with "The *yield return* statement in C# is potentially one of the most powerful and/or useful." My hope is that through the chapter you have learned how the **Filter**, **Sorter**, and **Selector** methods in *Linq* uses it so effectively. You can use that knowledge to your advantage making your applications more streamlined and efficient.

O(1) > O(N)

Most of the time when you are expressing an algorithm's complexity, that algorithm involves a collection. Therefore, when dealing with collections (*IEnumerable*), algorithmic complexity can be an issue. In the last chapter, we talked about *Linq* and the power that it offers when dealing with collections. That power and ease of use comes with a cost. If we don't take care while using *Linq*, we may introduce burdensome complexity.

Hopefully, you are familiar with Big-O notation, which provides a simple way of expressing the algorithmic complexity of code. Although this chapter won't detail all the specifics of calculating Big-O, before we dive into it, I want to lay some foundations.

Types of algorithmic complexity:

- $O(1)$, pronounced "Oh of one," is a constant time operation. For example, an $O(1)$ operation might obtain the value of a variable. Some collections do have constant time operations such as getting the value out of a *Dictionary* or *HashSet*.
- $O(\log n)$ is a logarithmic operation. With logarithmic operations, complexity increases with the size of the collection, but not in a 1:1 ratio. An example is doing a binary search of a tree.
- $O(n)$ is a linear operation. Complexity scales 1:1 with the size of the collection. Example: using a *foreach* loop.
- $O(n \log n)$ is slightly worse than $O(n)$. We're approaching the danger zone, but haven't gotten there yet. Common operations with this level of complexity include sorting a collection.
- $O(n^2)$, pronounced "Oh of n squared," is the danger zone. Complexity scales exponentially. You will rarely need this level of algorithmic complexity. Unfortunately, common examples of this may abound in your code base, most commonly as a nested *foreach* loop.

There are many more levels of complexity. Many, such as $O(n!)$, are worse than $O(n^2)$, but I'm not going to list them all out here. Instead, I'm going to focus on that big baddie of them all, $O(n^2)$. We will use the others as tools to help us avoid that nemesis of ours.

I'm also not going to say that you will never need very complex algorithms. Often, a company can do very well by solving complex problems efficiently, but even in those companies, those algorithms should be shielded and hidden from most of the application stack. In most of your day to day work, there is simply no need for that level of complexity. If a collection is big enough and it runs into an $O(n^2)$ operation, it will take an hour or multiple hours to run, stealing vital resources from the rest of your application.

In this chapter, we will use the books and categories concept from the previous chapter. It's a simple example showing a many-to-many relationship, which should make it easy to discuss. Before we go on, I want to make clear how I think about many of the algorithm choices we face in engineering every day.

Technically the books and categories are two different collections. Therefore, to be more explicit, we may say that an algorithm has O(n + m) complexity or O(n * m) complexity. I will be reducing those statements further by treating **n** and **m** the same, making the former O(n + m) into O(2n) or O(n), and the latter in to $O(n^2)$. Remember that in Big-O, constants are removed.

Many times, I've heard it said, "$O(n^2)$ is sufficient when the collection is small." While that can be true, I caution you to avoid it. What starts as a small collection can quickly grow out of control.

For example, perhaps you want to group a list of calendar events by day of the week. In this case, one of the two collections has a size of seven, the days of the week. Even in this example, seven is beginning to reach up into the danger zone.

Now imagine that you have a list of books containing 1,000,000 items, and well-defined hierarchy of thousands of categories. In this case, if we're not careful, operations can easily reach into the billions or beyond. If a single collection of 1,000,000 records is running through $O(n^2)$, operations reach into the trillions.

The worst example I've seen in my career was a table that had hundreds of thousands records and it ran into a $O(n^3)$ operation. Quadrillions of operations! That particular case was also doing disk access. In total, the operation took nearly two hours to complete. After re-evaluating the requirements, and a few days of refactoring, we were able to drop the processing time to less than 10 minutes.

You may be thinking, "So, if $O(n^2)$ algorithms are so dangerous, and my legacy code base may abound with them, why have they not been so troublesome to my company?" The simple answer comes down to hardware and test datasets.

In your lower environments, you may not have big robust hardware, but your test dataset may be smaller than what lives in production. Remember, we're talking about exponential complexity. Smaller data sets have exponentially smaller complexity.

Also, you may shrug off the performance issues in the test environment because test hardware doesn't come close to production hardware. When the code gets promoted to production, you never see the issues. This can easily happen especially when the production servers have four CPUs with 16 cores, each running over three Ghz with 128 GB of RAM. That is some serious hardware, and it can do a lot! Until it can't. Everything runs fine until Black Friday or the weekend of the big game or monthly reporting. Then, our exponential complexity rears its ugly head and it's all-hands-on-deck to figure out what brought down the production servers potentially meaning working long hours or into the weekend. Nobody wants that. That's what happened with the $O(n^3)$ operation I mentioned above. It ran fine, until it didn't.

I can hear your objection now: "My company has moved to the cloud. We don't have hardware issues." That may be true, but it is also a worse situation. The problem has simply moved from a hardware issue to a financial one. When you move to the cloud and start running cloud native solutions, the hardware costs are in CPU cycles. That $O(n^2)$ algorithm is now costing extra dollars every time it runs instead of once a year when you spin up new hardware. That affects the company's bottom line, your paycheck, and potentially your bonus.

Ok, now that we've discussed why $O(n^2)$ operations are so hazardous, let's learn how to identify and avoid them.

The easiest red flag to spot is a method signature that includes two different collection parameters.

```
 1  IEnumerable<Category> GetCategoriesFromBooks(
 2     IEnumerable<Book> books,
 3     IEnumerable<Category> categories)
 4  {
 5     List<Category> usedCategories = new List<Category>();
 6
 7     foreach (var book in books)
 8     {
 9        foreach (var catId in book.CategoryIds)
10        {
11           var category = categories.FirstOrDefault(c => c.ID == catId);
12           if (category != null &&
13              usedCategories.Any(uc => uc.ID == category.ID))
14           {
15              usedCategories.Add(category);
16           }
17        }
18     }
19     return usedCategories;
20  }
```

Any time you see nested *foreach* loops, chances are that you are looking at an O(n²) algorithm. The *foreach* itself is an O(n) operation. In English, this code translates to "for every operation, do another O(n) operation."

Now look closely at this code, there are more O(n) operations than the *foreach* statements. This is where *Linq* becomes dangerous. *Linq* makes complex operations easy to perform—so easy that we may not realize it. Both the calls to *FirstOrDefault* and *Any* are O(n) operations. In order to do that work, a collection must be iterated. This method has an O(n) to iterate the books, an O(n) operation to iterate the categories of each book, and two more O(n) operations inside. That means this method is O(n*n*2n). After removing the constant, this algorithm is O(n³).

You could argue that in this use case we must get all the categories from all the books. That means we must iterate all those collections from the *CategoryIds* property and there is no way around it. From that point of view, you could argue that the nested *foreach* statements are collectively doing a single O(n) operation, especially considering that the number of categories each book has is significantly smaller than the collection of all categories. Even viewed in this light, this method still has O(n²) complexity.

Let's look at how we can improve it.

```
 1  IEnumerable<Category> GetCategoriesFromBooks2(
 2      IEnumerable<Book> books,
 3      IEnumerable<Category> categories)
 4  {
 5      var usedCategoryIds = books.SelectMany(b => b.CategoryIds);
 6      var categoryHash = new HashSet<int>(usedCategoryIds);
 7
 8      foreach (var category in categories)
 9      {
10          if (categoryHash.Contains(category.ID))
11          {
12              yield return category;
13          }
14      }
15  }
```

In this example, we've used the *SelectMany* method from *Linq* to do the same work as the nested *foreach* statements, but then we did something interesting. We fed that new combined collection to a hash set. Why? Take a look at line 10. If we call *Contains* on a *List, Array,* or some other *IEnumerable*, it is an O(n) operation. Hash sets are different. Calling *Contains* on a *Hashset* is an *O(1)* operation, and we get O(1) operations for free when talking about algorithmic complexity. We have effectively turned nested *foreach* statements into two sequential *foreach* statements. In terms of Big-O, we've turned O(n²) into O(2n), which of course reduces to O(n).

The *Hashset* and its friend the *Dictionary* are two of the most useful tools in your toolbelt. Although I caution developers from using the *Linq* methods *ToList* and *ToArray*, I encourage the use of the *Linq* methods *ToDictionary* and *ToLookup*. Use them, and use them often. They will save your applications computational complexity over and over.

Hidden Complexity

Sometimes computational complexity is more subtle. In this example, we will look a common use case where we need to fetch items that are related through a many-to-many relationship. For this use case, the product owner has requested that when displaying a book on the site, that we also display a list of related books based on category. We will look for books with similar categories and sort them based on the number of common categories.

```
 1  public IEnumerable<Book> GetRelatedBooks(Book book)
 2  {
 3      Dictionary<Book, int> bookCounts = new Dictionary<Book, int>();
 4      foreach (var cat in _categoryProvider.GetCategories(book))
 5      {
 6          var booksInCat = _bookProvider.GetBooksInCategory(cat.ID);
 7          UpdateBookCounts(bookCounts, booksInCat);
 8      }
 9
10      return bookCounts.OrderBy(kvp => kvp.Value).Select(kvp => kvp.Key);
11  }
12
13  private static void UpdateBookCounts(
14      Dictionary<Book, int> bookCounts, IEnumerable<Book> books)
15  {
16      foreach (var relatedBook in books)
17      {
18          if (bookCounts.ContainsKey(relatedBook))
19          {
20              bookCounts[relatedBook] = bookCounts[relatedBook] + 1;
21          }
22          else
23          {
24              bookCounts[relatedBook] = 1;
25          }
26      }
27  }
28  }
```

Here we have two methods. The first method takes in a single book. No red flag there. It has a single *foreach* loop and a sort operation at the end that runs in $O(n \log n)$. That's still fine. The second method takes in a *Dictionary* and a collection of books. That's two collections; should we be worried?

When we inspect the contents of *UpdateBookCounts* we find that there is a single loop where all operations inside are $O(1)$. As a whole, it operates in $O(n)$ time. So, no red flag there either.

Yet *GetRelatedBooks* operates with $O(n^2)$ complexity. Why? Because for every iteration of the loop in *GetRelatedBooks*, we created another collection—and we had an $O(n)$ operation on *that* collection. Computational complexity carries down the stack. Even though the *foreach* statements are not physically nested in the layout of the file, at execution time, they are nested in the call stack.

In your code base, those two methods may exist in different classes, libraries, or even applications. Fixing this issue will take more work. We might have to revisit the question of how we determine what a related book is. We may also find that doing a *JOIN* in SQL may be a better solution. In the $O(n^3)$ example I mentioned, fixing that two-hour-long process included creating a new database table. Some problems are harder to solve than others.

Know thy tools

Some call it computer science; I call it art. As engineers, we are craftsman. We ply our trade, building infrastructures that enable people to do amazing things. When presented with a problem, we create solutions.

Like a structural engineer building a bridge or a sculptor creating a masterpiece, we have tools. And like any craftsperson, our tools dictate our solutions. Knowing how to use those tools, and more importantly, knowing which tool to reach for, is critical to our success. Should we reach for a hammer or a screwdriver? Maybe we need a bulldozer. Maybe we need a scalpel.

Using a bulldozer is fun, but they are expensive and used as a last resort when other measures simply will not do. We all want to work on green-field projects where we get to build systems from the ground up. The reality is that we rarely receive that opportunity. Most of the time we work within some existing structure.

If you ask a developer what tools they use, they will likely list things like Visual Studio and Notepad++. Those are in a category of tools called integrated development environment (IDE), but there are so many more categories. Would you put a bulldozer and a screwdriver in the same category? Let's take a look at the many categories of tools and how we can use them to our advantage.

Integrated Development Environments (IDEs)

As a C# developer, chances are you use Visual Studio, Visual Studio Code, or one of a few other choices. Whichever you choose, make sure you know how to efficiently use it. I love showing junior developers what happens when they type *"ctor, tab, tab"* in Visual Studio, or when they change a method name and press *"ctrl + ."* or when they type out a method call to a method that doesn't exist and doing the same key stroke. The look on their face when they realize the potential of their IDE is priceless.

There are many other IDEs to know as well. They may not be traditionally called an IDE, but they are things that you do integrate into your development. When working with regular expressions, I absolutely love Expresso. When working with git, you should know the command line, but having a UI can be extremely helpful. My personal favorite is Git Extensions, but there are many choices. Choosing an IDE and knowing how to use it efficiently will save you hundreds of hours.

Data Structures

Lists, arrays, dictionaries, queues, red-black trees, and *IEnumerable* all have their uses. As seen in the last chapter, reaching for a *List* instead of a *Dictionary* can have disastrous consequences.

We may use a tree a bit less often, but when it's the right tool, don't be afraid to reach for it. They can be trickier to use because often we'll use a recursive algorithm with them. Sometimes there's no better choice. Unfortunately, .NET does not have many generic trees readily available. When a tree is needed, we may have to build it ourselves.

Craftspeople do this all the time. Often when a carpenter needs a jig, there's no good off-the-shelf solution. Most expert woodworkers find themselves building some sort of jig in many of their projects. Similarly, if you need a type of data structure and you've confirmed that no off-the-shelf version exists, make one for yourself. Watch out for reinventing the wheel—we engineers love to build it better than it has been done before.

So, to repeat, because it is that important: Look for an off-the-shelf tool first. If one doesn't exist to suit your needs, feel free to build what you do need.

Alogorithms

We already discussed how O(n2) can be a bad thing. Knowing what algorithms we can combine together allows us to avoid overly complex operations. Knowing what algorithm to use really comes down to understanding the problem. Once you truly understand the problem, you may find inspiration from previous experiences.

For example, when doing a binary search, you might reach for a tree, but experience can teach that you don't need one because, the *List<T>* class has a *BinarySearch* method. You must make sure the list is sorted, but you don't need a tree to do a binary search. Knowing that a binary search is the right algorithm is more important than knowing trees are good at them.

Libraries

Like a construction worker choosing a circular saw or miter saw, when it comes to libraries, there are many brands to choose from. Knowing the pros and cons of each can help us choose better tools. Knowing how a library can solve a problem is important also. Can I use a circular saw to cut trim and molding? Sure, but a miter saw is a better choice. Similarly, regex is amazing. Is it the right choice? Maybe; maybe not—it depends on the situation.

We can choose from among the many libraries at our disposal, including *Linq,* which we discussed in detail last chapter. When we are unit testing, we can use either *Moq* or *NSubstitute* for mocking. When choosing an IOC container, we can use *Microsoft.Extensions.Dependency-Injection*, *Autofac*, *Simple Injector*, or one of a dozen other choices.

Frameworks

When building out a web application, we still have to make a few choices. Should we use WCF or MVC? Should we use Winforms or WPF? Maybe we should choose Unity. Knowing what frameworks are available to you and their pros and cons help you build better experiences for other developers and ultimately your customers.

Wait Statements

It doesn't happen often, but sometimes our applications need to literally wait and do nothing until some event happens or time elapses. I remember as a child programming a Commodore 64. One of the first things I learned after learning the basic (literally BASIC) *if* and *for* statements was a concept of a *wait* statement. Back then, it was a simple *for* loop that did nothing inside. You changed the length of the delay by changing the number of iterations. That seems silly today. Oddly, we still struggle with this simple concept today.

C# offers numerous options for waiting. The most basic is *Thread.Sleep()*. Back in the days of BASIC, when applications weren't multi-threaded, this would have been a very handy tool. It's perfect if you have only one thread and you need it to wait.

Today's applications are much different. Threads are commodities with value. Telling a thread to sleep wastes one of your valuable commodities. Please do not reach for that tool. Like the *for* loop, there are many better options.

If you need to wait for a short time, you can choose from among a few different *Timer* classes depending on your needs. They have options to automatically reset or be interrupted. If you need to wait a long time, you can choose from many scheduling libraries, including something like Hangfire.

Sometimes you need to wait until some condition is met. You may be tempted to write *while(conditionIsNotMet)*. Again, there are many better options. Today's processors run very fast. That *while* loop will run millions of times in a very short order. For the environmentally conscience, understand that a *while(true)* statement is increasing your application's carbon footprint a lot as you cook the processor.

Alternately, instead of a *while(true)* statement, consider the *SpinWait* class for short delays or the *EventWaitHandle* class for longer delays. Both will allow you to wait until a condition.

If your delay is on the order of minutes or even seconds, you may consider a different approach altogether. Instead of waiting for another process to send you data, consider creating an event to handle that situation. It's the same difference as pushing data through a system versus polling a system for data. In almost all cases, pushing is better than polling.

In the Task Parallel Library (TPL), we have *Task.Delay()*. It is not much different from *Thread.Sleep()*, but a whole lot nicer to your thread pool. In the next chapter, we will talk about one of the most complex tools available to a C# developer, the TPL.

We have many types of tools at our disposal. Knowing all the types of tools, what they do, and how to use them is what allows us to turn science into art. The number and combination of tools we have with our tools is infinite. Go make something beautiful.

Awaiting means not waiting

Humans are notoriously bad at multi-tasking. Studies have shown that when we try to multi-task, we have a measurable drop in IQ. We can combine tasks that do not require extra thought. For example: breathing and walking. But for tasks that require coordination of multiple faculties we do not fare so well. Imagine reciting multiplication tables while playing speed chess.

On the other hand, computers are great at multitasking. Because this kind of processing does not come naturally to us, when we attempt to tackle the problem of executing multiple threads, we often get it wrong. Even when we get it right, it is usually on a very small scale. Let's take a look at another book example.

On our bookselling website, when a user lands on a page for a specific book we need to display many pieces of information. We may want to show other books by the same author. While the book may have many categories, perhaps it has a primary category, and we want to show other books with the same primary category. In our MVC or API controller we might have code that looks like this:

```
1 object GetPageInfo(int bookId)
2 {
3    var book = _bookProvider.GetById(bookId);
4    var booksByAuthor = _bookProvider.GetByAuthor(book.AuthorId);
5    var booksInCategory = _bookProvider.GetTop10BooksInCategory(
6       book.PrimaryCategoryId);
7
8    return new {
9       booksByAuthor,
10      booksInCategory
11   };
12 }
```

 Some of you got to line 8 and cringed when you saw the formatting. That line represents what is being returned in a JSON payload. As such, it is formatted like JavaScript. Through your career, you're going to come across a lot of different formatting styles. If you get hung up on every formatting inconsistency you see, you're going to spend a lot of time fixing things that aren't broken. Get used to reading code by other contributors. It may help you understand their intent and, in turn, understand the code a little more.

This is a pretty straightforward method, but when we think about what it is doing under the hood, we can make some improvements. Lines 3 through 5 all make calls to the database. Lines 4 and 5 could be run simultaneously. Both the database and the operating system can easily multitask. This is where using multiple threads can help. Let's look at one old-school way of achieving this.

```
 1  object GetPageInfo2(int bookId)
 2  {
 3      var book = _bookProvider.GetById(bookId);
 4      IEnumerable<Book> booksByAuthor = null;
 5      IEnumerable<Book> booksInCategory = null;
 6      Thread authorThread = new Thread(() =>
 7          booksByAuthor = _bookProvider.GetByAuthor(book.AuthorId)
 8      );
 9      authorThread.Start();
10      Thread catThread = new Thread(() =>
11          booksInCategory =
12          _bookProvider.GetTop10BooksInCategory(book.PrimaryCategoryId)
13      );
14      catThread.Start();
15      authorThread.Join();
16      catThread.Join();
17
18      return new
19      {
20          booksByAuthor,
21          booksInCategory
22      };
23  }
```

What a mess! We did achieve better efficiency, but at the cost of significant additional complexity. This code does not handle exceptions, and in this old-school way of doing things, exception handling would introduce even more complexity.

There are other opportunities to make this code efficient. Line 3 is still waiting for a database call to complete, and while we did create two new threads to execute simultaneously, the thread we're on is still sitting and waiting on lines 15 and 16. Fortunately, there is another way.

Way back in 2011, inspired by F# asynchronous workflows, C# introduced *async/await*.

While these were certainly not the first times asynchronous programming models were introduced, they were arguably the first to do it well at scale by using language features to make it seamless instead of consuming libraries. Since then, its adoption has been incredible, and other languages have raced to stay in feature parity.

To use *async* and *await*, there are some rules you must follow:

1. You cannot use *await* if your method is not marked with *async*.
2. When writing an *async* method, you should nearly always, if not always, return a *Task* or *Task<T>*.

 A note on returning a *Task* versus returning a *Task<T>*: If your *async* method would normally return *void*, you should return a *Task* instead. Otherwise, you return *Task<T>*. The compiler will let you return *void* with an *async* method, but I am not going to cover that very exceptional use case here. In fact, I am advocating that you DON'T DO IT.

Now that we've laid out the ground rules, let's take a look at how we can improve our method.

```
1 async Task<object> GetPageInfoAsync(int bookId)
2 {
3     var book = await _bookProvider.GetByIdAsync(bookId);
4     var booksByAuthor = _bookProvider.GetByAuthorAsync(book.AuthorId);
5     var booksInCategory = _bookProvider
6         .GetTop10BooksInCategoryAsync(book.PrimaryCategoryId);
7
8     return new {
9         booksByAuthor = await booksByAuthor,
10        booksInCategory = await booksInCategory
11    };
12 }
```

It really is that easy. This method is nearly identical to the first with a little *Task*, *async*, and *await* decoration. Let's go through it line by line.

Right from the beginning of line 1, we added the *async* keyword. This tells the compiler that asynchronous operations are about to begin, so it should prepare all that nastiness of working with threads that we don't want to do. We are also returning a *Task<object>* instead of *object*.

On line 3, we added the very special *await* keyword. When that line executes, the common language runtime (CLR) is instructed that processes can use the current thread for other things until the *Task* being awaited has completed. Other processes needing a thread can now use this thread from the thread pool until it is needed again.

While the title of this chapter is "Awaiting means not waiting," it may be more accurate to say "Awaiting means not making others wait." From the context of the thread itself, though, it doesn't need to wait and can get other things done.

This simple construct has allowed us to take advantage of a computer's ability to multi-task. By itself, this line may not save the application much. In fact, it is actually doing more work to help us. When we use it as a matter of habit, however, the CPU spends less time idly waiting for tasks to complete. Our overall hardware utilization increases dramatically, especially in a scenario like a web application where we handle requests from thousands or more users simultaneously.

Lines 4 and 5 are both returning a *Task*. However, we did not *await* them. If we did, we would be running them sequentially while introducing the complexity of thread management. By not awaiting them, we allow them to run concurrently.

Finally, we *await* them on lines 9 and 10. If we really wanted to squeeze out performance, we may consider using *Task.WhenAll()* to await them both at the same time. We may want to do that anyway to aid in exception handling. After they return, we can inspect the *Exception* property of each *Task*.

 The *Task* class has several static methods that I encourage you to explore. It also has several instance members you should become familiar with such as *Exception, Start(),* and *Wait()*. One that I have found particularly handy is *ContinueWith()*.

ConfigureAwait(false)

Old-school WinForm developers know the pain of interacting with the user interface thread—the dreaded "UI thread." When multi-threading, there are times you need to synchronize your threads. One example of that found earlier in this chapter is when we called *authorThread.Join()*. WinForms require some synchronization when interacting with the UI. So, if you need to change the text of a button or the contents of a drop-down menu, you need to make sure you are working on the UI thread.

The *SynchronizationContext* was added to aid these types of tasks. By default, a *Task* will attempt to synchronize. When working in .NET Framework (traditional .NET) and dealing with a UI thread, this is incredibly handy. The *Task* tries to protect you from blowing up the UI. Unfortunately, that protection comes with a cost. The cost of synchronizing threads is demonstrated above by *authorThread.Join()*. There are many times however you don't need to worry about synchronizing threads. When working in .NET Framework and you don't have a UI thread or *SynchronizationContext* to worry about, in order to override the default behavior, you must call *ConfigureAwait(false)*. That *false* tells the CLR not to synchronize and allows work to continue on the first available thread. In our most recent example, all three lines would have *ConfigureAwait(false)* appended to them.

> ❗ Anytime you see a class name with the suffix "Context," be aware that turbulent waters may lay ahead. Whether that is *SynchronizationContext, HttpContext, Domain-Context,* or *DbContext*, almost all "context" type objects are associated with a larger idea of state that is hard to manage. If you find yourself wanting to write a *Context* object, it may be a sign that you are trying to do too much, possibly breaking the single responsibility principle. Often, their static nature can become troublesome too.

The .NET core framework did away with the *SychronizationContext,* so modern applications don't have to deal with it. If you are working in .NET standard, however, your library could be consumed by either by a .NET Framework application or a .NET Core application. Since your consumer may be dealing with a *SynchronizationContext* you must also.

To async or not to async

Remember that if your method is *async*, you should always return a *Task*. But what about the inverse: If I am returning a *Task,* should I also mark the method *async*? The short answer is, "maybe." Remember all that work we did when manually creating threads? Well, when you mark a method *async* the compiler is going to spend significant resources that you may or may not want to spend. If you can return the *Task* without the *await*, you will save your application some work. Somebody will eventually have to *await* the *Task*, but that person does not need to be you.

Here's an overly simplified example.

```
1 async Task<bool> DoWork()
2 {
3     return await Task.Run(() => true);
4 }
5
6 Task<bool> DoWorkFixed()
7 {
8     return Task.Run(() => true);
9 }
```

In our previous example, we had to wait for the first database call to get the book before continuing. We did need to *await*. The first rule or our two rules above is that if we are going to *await*, we must also use *async*. Therefore, we needed to use the *async* keyword. However, if the last line of your method starts with *return await*, chances are you don't need to use *async*. There can be complications with other things that have their own context like a *SqlConnection* object that will try to get in your way. You may find that the connection has closed when the caller goes to do the *await* and get the task's *Result*. There is no hard rule here except to say that if you can return the *Task* without the *async/await*, you should.

To Task or not to Task

The first time you start working with *async/await*, you may feel the pain of trying to deal with a method that returns asynchronously when called from a synchronous process. You may also feel this pain when incorporating newer libraries into older code that were written before *async/await* was introduced.

I feel your pain. You cannot call *await* from a method that is not marked *async*. So, what do you do if your MVC controller action is not *async*? Nowadays, the easy thing is to mark your controller *async*, provided it is using a version that supports *async*.

What if you're working in the business layer and trying to call your new data access layer which is utilizing newer *async* abilities? Now you need to mark your business logic layer with *async*. That also means changing the method signature to return a *Task*. But changing the signature method breaks unit tests, and you still need to go update the controller, possibly creating the same issues. Ouch!

Now that you understand the conundrum, you may be tempted to have all new methods return *Task* or *Task<T>*. I caution you to not form that habit. To take a quote from my favorite Star Trek film, "Let us redefine progress to mean that just because we can do a thing, it does not necessarily follow that we must."

The *async* keyword comes with cost. When we use *async*, we are explicitly telling the compiler to manage threads. If all your operations are executing locally, you should not use the *async* keyword. Sure, your operation may take a while, but the CPU is not waiting for something to complete; it stays busy. Adding *async* in that case only adds the complexity of thread management when it is not needed. Now, if you know your business layer is going to be waiting on a call the data access layer, you should mark it *async* to keep the chain going.

Here is my general rule: If you are serializing or deserializing, you should use *async*. Whether that serialization is to disk, database, HTTP call, message queue, or any other operation that leaves your local memory, you should use *async*. Otherwise, don't. Save your application some extra compute cycles.

No Test == No Proof

If I told you, "My pig learned to fly the other day," you would want some pretty compelling proof. Equally, if a developer says to a product owner, "All the numbers in the half-dozen columns on this multi-page report are correct," the product owner is going to want proof, and they are going to want it every time any feature is added. In other words, they are going to want **regression testing**.

As I mentioned in the preface of the book, a decade ago, many companies' automated testing standards were not what they are today. I once heard, "Why do we need to write a bunch of unit tests? That's why we hire QA folks." The idea of saving money by not writing tests is continually being challenged. Fortunately, automated tests consistently prove their worth. That all being said, if you don't put careful thought into an overall testing strategy, maintaining the tests can become more expensive than maintaining the code.

In the history of computing, sometimes ideas take a while to ferment. At one point, mainframes with thin clients were the way to go. Then local computing power increased, and applications could do more locally, including database processing (for example, Access Database). Then came the web, and processing moved back to servers, with browsers serving as the thin client. Slowly, the industry is settling on single page applications (SPA), where the bulk of rendering logic is done on the client and the server manages data. That's where we are today—but I wouldn't be surprised if it changed again.

In some regards, when it comes to testing, the industry is still playing that back-and-forth game. I think we all agree by now that automated testing is a good thing, but what kinds of tests should we have? What does it mean when someone says "integration test"?

In this chapter, I'm going to talk about five different types of test and what they mean to me. Then I'll talk about what I consider an ideal strategy for testing and why I think it works so well. You may have different ideas. That's fine. This is certainly an area where new ideas are sure to keep changing how we view testing. Before diving into the details of the five types of test I've chosen to discuss, let's get some context into how they play a role in our overall testing strategy.

The Testing Triangle

I didn't invent the idea of a testing triangle, but I find it very helpful when discussing an overall testing strategy. The premise is simple: The most expensive tests sit at the top of the triangle. They do have value, but the cost per test is great. You should have the fewest number of those tests. The cheapest tests sit at the base of the triangle. Because they have the least infrastructure, time constraints, and cost, they provide the greatest value per test. Therefore, they should represent the bulk of your testing strategy.

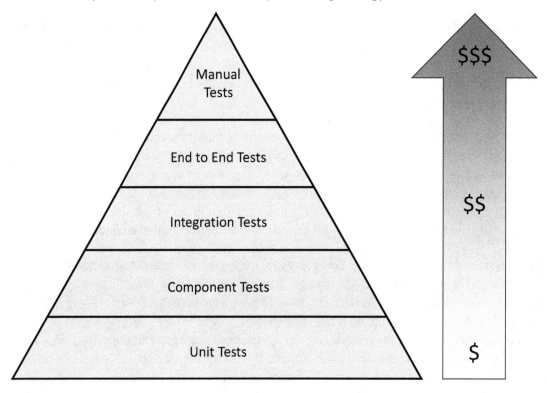

Some organizations may not have a testing triangle. They may have a testing hourglass, or worse, an inverted triangle.

The triangle is a guide to help you with your overall strategy and see where your testing efforts may need improvement. The triangle I've created here has five layers, but perhaps yours only has three or six. In some organizations that have traditionally not used many automated tests, the testing triangle can be exceptionally useful for talking about tests as an organization and helping you communicate what you would like to see in the overall strategy.

Now that we have some context, let's dive into the details of each type of test represented in my version of the testing triangle.

Manual Tests

Manual tests require a human to execute them. For example, a company may have a pre-defined list of steps to test individual use cases. The tester then follows the instructions in the list to verify the application is behaving as intended.

These are the most expensive kinds of tests because every test run uses person-hours. However, the benefit is that these tests have a nearly zero likelihood of false positive results.

From here on out, we'll talk about tests through the lens of automated testing. That doesn't mean these other types couldn't be manual, just that some are more likely to be automated. Could a manual test be an end-to-end test? Yes absolutely, and they likely are. Can an automated test be an end-to-end test? Sure, but in the scope of all automated tests, it likely isn't.

End-to-end tests

End-to-end tests exist to test the entire system. If the application is receiving information from a message bus, which had its messages created by a user on another site, has a distributed cache, and writes to a database, an automated end-to-end test would execute all those code paths.

Testers often use a common browser automation framework called Selenium for end-to-end testing. You may have heard the term "Selenium tests" thrown around the office.

This type of testing is expensive to maintain. It usually requires a separate environment that humans don't interact with, so that the data stays consistent, preventing people from accidentally breaking a test and creating false negatives. Automated tests exist to help us constantly regression test our product. When a test breaks, a human being must go fix it, and what is the point of having broken tests?

Additionally, because these tests have the greatest number of moving parts, they are both the most fragile and the most difficult to troubleshoot. As a result, these tests tend to have the most false negatives, which leads to more man-hours spent troubleshooting and fixing.

Integration Tests

The broadest definition of an integration test is a test that crosses an application boundary. That boundary could be between two systems like the application and the database, or the client and the application. It could also be a boundary between architectural layers like the business and data access layers. That is why this definition is too broad for me. It is however a very helpful definition in that it clearly defines tests that are not unit tests, discussed in detail below.

I define an integration test as any test that tests the integration of any two stand-alone parts of the application stack. That could be browser to application, application to database, message bus to application, or... you get the idea.

While an end-to-end test is a type of integration test, to me, an integration test is smaller in scope than an end-to-end test. We want these tests to answer the question, "Can the two systems integrate?" We don't want to test every use case.

Integration tests are also somewhat expensive, because like the end-to-end tests, they may require dedicated infrastructure. Although more robust than end-to-end tests, integration tests also have a fair number of moving parts, making them somewhat fragile.

Integration tests and end-to-end tests may or may not live in the same project. Perhaps your organization has several teams working on microservices and each team has a suite of integration tests, but another team is responsible for the overall health of the system. They run the end-to-end tests. That would mean for your team you have a testing trapezoid.

Component tests

Of the tests we discussed so far, these are the first that do not require additional infrastructure. Because of that, they cost significantly less and are inherently more valuable.

These will often take the form of some sort of scenario test (not discussed here) that verifies multiple steps a user would take in some scenario.

Component tests fall into two categories: First, somewhat like the integration tests discussed above, a component test checks a scenario where one part of the application talks to another part of the application. Second, you can use component tests for objects that rely on state, such as a data-structure. For example, it is nearly impossible to test the *Dequeue* method of a *Queue* class without first testing the *Enqueue* method. Conversely, you cannot test the validity of the *Enqueue* method without testing the *Dequeue*.

In most of the code I write, there are actually only a few component tests. I use component test when unit tests don't make sense, and they actually live in the same project with my unit tests. So, from that regard, they get lumped into the same category.

Unit tests

The broadest definition of a unit test is a test which verifies the smallest unit possible. What if your *aspx* page is doing data access? (May the universe help you if that is the case.) Well, then the smallest unit will also require an end-to-end test. For me, a unit test is a test that verifies a single method.

These tests offer the greatest value per unit. Because they test extremely small units, they can run hundreds of times per day with little infrastructure cost. Also, because they have the least number of other components needed, they are the most stable. If one of these tests break, it is likely because a refactor did not account for some special use case.

Additionally, developers can run thousands of unit tests in mere minutes before a check-in. Running unit tests consistently uncovers bugs earlier in the software development lifecycle (SDLC), saving many person-hours. Unfortunately, your legacy code may be structured so that unit testing is not possible.

Many of the maxims in this book are here in part to help ensure that you can write unit tests for the code. When developers don't follow the maxims laid out in this book, the best you can hope for is component tests—and maybe not even then.

Code Coverage

When discussing overall testing strategy, you should also consider code coverage. Often, when we talk about code coverage and what gets reported, we are only discussing unit tests. I aim for at least 90% coverage for unit tests, but honestly, when you follow the maxims in this book, you can easily achieve 95% code coverage. But even if we achieve close to 100% test coverage, there can still be gaps.

The diagram below shows, at a high level, the application stack from a web page to the application with all its components to the database. The lines at the bottom represent what gets covered. Not all possible combination of lines is shown.

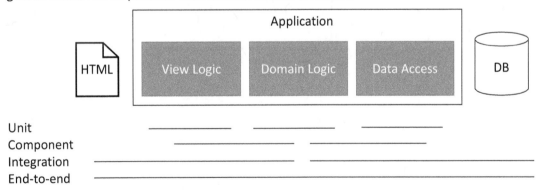

As you can see, even robust unit tests with 100% code coverage would still leave gaps. The unit tests will test that any individual component is doing what it should, but it does not prove that the different components within the application can function together as a whole. Any conversation about your organization's overall testing strategy should take that into account.

Perhaps you've been told that you must have end-to-end tests and 90% code coverage on unit tests. In that scenario, you may not have the man hours to maintain a full suite of integration tests as well. Or perhaps you find end-to-end tests to be too expensive and therefore opt for a robust set of integration tests while manually verifying end-to-end tests. In either case, only having unit tests is not sufficient, and only having integration tests will not cover all the edge cases, unless you have a large number of them, which is not cost effective. Finding the right balance is up to you and your organization.

Dependencies Lacking Injection are Fixed Anchors

Now that we have reviewed types of tests and code coverage, let's discuss the tests that we should use most often: unit tests. The following three chapters will focus on how to write quality unit tests and unit testable code.

If you are dealing with a large legacy code base with a lot of anchors, writing these kinds of tests might not be possible. That's okay. You'll still find lots of good information here to help you think about how to test and to understand the scope of the tests you do write.

For the example, we will use the domain logic layer of an order system for a fictitious e-commerce site.

Part of our job as developers is to provide value to the organization where we work. I will often, when talking about code, talk about the value it offers. We can offer exceptional value by getting 95% code coverage. That last 5% can be difficult, will take more time, and hence be less valuable.

In the domain logic layer, this value increases even more. If we work for a business, that is where the company makes its money and your paycheck. We might call it the business logic layer instead of domain logic. Your company doesn't make money by saving information to a database or processing HTTP requests. Yes, they happen to use those technologies, but their value as a business comes from the products and services they offer.

As a developer who takes pride in my work, I find that insufficient code coverage on the business logic to be just that—insufficient. Let's take a look at how well-structured code makes writing tests with 95+% code coverage easy, and we'll do it with meaningful assertions.

The following code example represents the code we will be testing. It is a class that orchestrates the processing of an order on the e-commerce site. It only has one method named *PlaceOrder*. That method will be the singular unit that we test. It takes in an *Order* model, validates that all the information is correct, and if it is valid, saves that order to another system for continued processing.

```
1  public class OrderLogic : IOrderLogic
2  {
3     readonly IOrderValidator _validator;
4     readonly IOrderProvider _orderProvider;
5     readonly ILogger _logger;
6
7     public OrderLogic(IOrderValidator validator,
8        IOrderProvider orderProvider, ILogger logger)
9     {
10       _validator = validator;
11       _orderProvider = orderProvider;
12       _logger = logger;
13    }
14
15    public async Task<IEnumerable<OrderValidationError>> PlaceOrder(Order order)
16    {
17       var errors = await _validator.ValidateOrder(order);
18
19       if (errors.Any())
20       {
21          _logger.Log("Cannot process order");
22          return errors;
23       }
24
25       await _orderProvider.SaveOrder(order);
26
27       return errors;
28    }
29 }
```

So, what about those anchors? You can see that the class has three dependencies that are injected by interface. It doesn't have any anchors. Those interfaces will help us to make this unit test truly a unit test. When we are testing a method does what it should, we do not need to test that its dependency is doing what it should. If the validator was not injected, our tests for the *OrderLogic* class would be anchored to the *OrderValidator*. Our unit test, even if it did not make any assertions on the validator, would still be required to execute code in the validator.

We use mocking to ensure our test itself is also not anchored to a dependency. My personal favorite mocking framework is *Moq*, which we'll use here. Other robust mocking frameworks will provide similar features. We will be using XUnit as our testing framework.

Unit tests are often arranged into three steps: **arrange**, **act**, and **assert**. We'll spend the rest of this chapter on **arrange**, then review **act** and **assert** in the following chapters.

Arrange

The **arrange** section of the test sets up the conditions or use case we intend to verify. We need to test at least two conditions in our method: when errors exist and when they do not. For our first test, we will test when errors do exist.

First, we set up our dependencies, or arrange the test.

```
1 //arrange
2 Mock<IOrderValidator> mockValidator = new Mock<IOrderValidator>();
3 Mock<IOrderProvider> mockProvider = new Mock<IOrderProvider>();
4 Mock<ILogger> mockLogger = new Mock<ILogger>();
```

Next, we instruct the dependencies to behave in the manner that will cause our use case to happen. Specifically, we need to tell the mocked validator to return at least one validation error.

```
1 mockValidator.Setup(v => v.ValidateOrder(It.IsAny<Order>()))
2     .ReturnsAsync(new OrderValidationError[] {
3       new OrderValidationError()
4       {
5           Message = "Live long and prosper"
6       }
7   });
```

"Live long and prosper"!? What is that? Well, it's a mocked validation message. I often put fun little snippets into my tests. Our logic class doesn't care what the validation message is. It only cares that it got one or more errors. If you come across an integer value in a test I wrote, chances are, it is 1701 because I like Star Trek and that is the registry number of the starship *Enterprise*. Besides, sometimes writing tests can seem like a chore. So, why not make it fun?

On a more serious note, this also helps to ensure our unit tests are in fact unit tests. I can't tell you the number of times I've seen "unit tests" that were not unit tests because they were passed a real-world value and the dependency used that to call another system. By passing fictitious values, we ensure our unit tests remain unit tests.

This is another place where the anchor would show itself. If the validator were not injected, we could not mock it. We would not be able to instruct it to behave correctly. Instead, we would be forced to put in an order that the validator would need to produce the desired result. Setting up an order to have validation errors might entail digging into that class to understand its logic. The testing for our order orchestration would be dragged down by needing to understand in detail another part of the system.

The last thing to do in our **arrange** section is to get an instance of the thing we are trying to test.

```
1  var logicUnderTest = new OrderLogic(
2      mockValidator.Object,
3      mockProvider.Object,
4      mockLogger.Object);
```

That one line makes it clear that our dependencies are injected. They are not anchors. Now our use case is set up and we are ready to execute.

In the next chapter, we'll talk about the **act** phase of a unit test.

Tested anchors prove not boats float

In the previous section, we discussed unit tests and the **arrange** step in creating a unit test. Here we'll take a moment to explore executing unit tests in the **act** step.

Executing the tests for the *OrderLogic* class should not execute any code inside the validator. Validator unit tests are responsible for testing the validator. If our *OrderLogic* tests do execute code in the validator, and there is a problem inside the validator, it would break our test, leading to a false negative result. Acting like an anchor, it would be a drag on our development efforts.

Act

Here is the **act** section of our test.

```
1 //act
2 var result = await logicUnderTest.PlaceOrder(new Order());
```

One line? Yep, one line. If the **act** portion of our test is more than one line, odds are we aren't writing a unit test. That may be our intent. If we were testing a data structure, like a queue, the **act** portion of our test would likely call both the *Enqueue* and *Dequeue* methods. As mentioned earlier, that would be a component test. In this chapter, we are focusing on unit tests that test a single method. One line is all we need.

Because we took the time for thoughtful design, this line was not painful. If the validator was constructed inside the *OrderLogic* class, this one line would have executed the validation logic as well (testing the anchor). Our test would not be a unit test. At the very least, it would be a component test, and at worst, it might be an integration test.

Empty assertions are blankets holding no heat.

Blankets cover you. But a blanket full of holes doesn't do its job well; you might as well not have a blanket. Similarly, your tests provide code coverage. A test without assertions is like a blanket full of holes. It provides code coverage but doesn't do what it is supposed to do. Instead, it only gives you a false sense of security.

In the previous section, we discussed unit tests and the **act** step in creating a unit test. Here we'll take a moment to explore executing unit tests in the **assert** step.

Assert

In this use case we can expect a couple things to happen. First, the *OrderLogic* class will call the *logger*.

```
1 mockLogger.Verify(l => l.Log(It.IsAny<string>()));
```

I have seen tests where the only assertion was that the logger was called with an explicit message. I find two things wrong with that.

First, a business rarely cares about the log message format. Later, when a more explicit log message is written, it breaks the test, and we must go fix the test. In my opinion, it is fine to verify the logger should be called, but what actually gets logged isn't so important. That is why I used *It.IsAny<string>()* instead of the more explicit *"Cannot process order."*

 There may be a valid business use case for having an explicit message sent to the logging system. If our e-commerce company is forward-thinking, they may have a requirement to send the validation error messages to a telemetry system, allowing them to identify the most common errors to help make better user experience (UX). In that case, we should be more explicit in our assertion.

Second, having only a single assertion that a log was written is virtually meaningless. We need quality assertions to have quality coverage.

```
1 Assert.Single(result);
2 var error = result.First();
3 Assert.Equal("Live long and prosper", error.Message);
```

If I didn't care about the log message, why do I care about the validation message? We are trying to verify the correctness of our unit. If our unit did not return what the validator gave us, our unit would be incorrect. That's why we care about this message.

Lastly, assertions I often find missing from tests are the assertions of what our code **didn't** do. In this case, we do not want to save the order because the order is invalid. We should assert that we did **not** save a bad order.

```
1 mockProvider.Verify(p => p.SaveOrder(It.IsAny<Order>()), Times.Never);
```

Now we have a quality test, and our blanket does hold heat. Here is what the whole test class that includes a test for when there are no validation errors may look like.

```
 1 public class OrderLogicTests
 2 {
 3    [Fact]
 4    public async Task WhenValidationErrorsExist_ReturnsErrorsAndDoesNotSave()
 5    {
 6       //arrange
 7       Mock<IOrderValidator> mockValidator = new Mock<IOrderValidator>();
 8       Mock<IOrderProvider> mockProvider = new Mock<IOrderProvider>();
 9       Mock<ILogger> mockLogger = new Mock<ILogger>();
10
11       mockValidator.Setup(v => v.ValidateOrder(It.IsAny<Order>()))
12          .ReturnsAsync(new OrderValidationError[] {
13             new OrderValidationError()
14             {
15                Message = "Live long and prosper"
16             }
17          });
18
19       var logicUnderTest = new OrderLogic(
20          mockValidator.Object,
21          mockProvider.Object,
22          mockLogger.Object);
23
24       //act
25       var result = await logicUnderTest.PlaceOrder(new Order());
26
27       //assert
28       mockLogger.Verify(l => l.Log(It.IsAny<string>()));
29       Assert.Single(result);
```

```
30      var error = result.First();
31      Assert.Equal("Live long and prosper", error.Message);
32
33      mockProvider.Verify(p => p.SaveOrder(It.IsAny<Order>()), Times.Never);
34  }
35
36  [Fact]
37  public async Task WhenNoValidationErrors_SavesOrder()
38  {
39    //arrange
40    Mock<IOrderValidator> mockValidator = new Mock<IOrderValidator>();
41    Mock<IOrderProvider> mockProvider = new Mock<IOrderProvider>();
42    Mock<ILogger> mockLogger = new Mock<ILogger>();
43
44    mockValidator.Setup(v => v.ValidateOrder(It.IsAny<Order>()))
45      .ReturnsAsync(Enumerable.Empty<OrderValidationError>());
46
47    var fakeOrder = new Order();
48
49    var logicUnderTest = new OrderLogic(
50      mockValidator.Object,
51      mockProvider.Object,
52      mockLogger.Object);
53
54    //act
55    var result = await logicUnderTest.PlaceOrder(fakeOrder);
56
57    //assert
58    Assert.Empty(result);
59    mockProvider.Verify(p => p.SaveOrder(fakeOrder), Times.Once);
60  }
61 }
```

If you ran a code coverage report for these two tests, you would find that the *OrderLogic* class has 100% coverage!

Also notice that no other classes have any coverage. The only exception, depending on your coverage tool, will be the properties in the *Order* model. This means that our unit tests are, in fact, unit tests. These are not integration tests or component tests. Thoughtful design does make testing easy!

Empty assertions are blankets holding no heat.

new is a four-letter word

Of all the maxims on the list, this one perhaps draws the most scrutiny. Do I think that *new* is a curse word? Yes, absolutely. Do I think that you should never use curse words? No, but I do believe in using the right word for the job. You have to know when they are and are not appropriate to successfully use them.

Why do I believe *new* is a dirty keyword? It allocates memory. It consumes system resources. When we allocate memory, eventually we must deallocate it. Excessive use of *new* creates excessive work for the *Garbage Collector*. See, garbage! When we litter our code with *new*, we are wasteful.

Given that *new* is a key(curse)word we must use in C#, let's make sure we use it correctly.

To make this analogy a little clearer, let's take an example from our chapter on *IEnumerable* and replace the *new* curse-word with a different four-letter word.

```
 1  static void Main(string[] args)
 2  {
 3      AccountParsingLogic logic = crap AccountParsingLogic();
 4
 5      Func<string[], Account> lineParser = cells => {
 6          var id = logic.GetAccountNumber(cells[0]);
 7          var name = logic.GetNameForSaving(cells[1]);
 8          var value = logic.GetValue(cells[2]);
 9
10          if (id.HasValue)
11          {
12              return crap Account()
13              {
14                  ID = id.Value,
15                  Name = name,
16                  Value = value
17              };
18          }
19          return null;
20      };
21
22      var csvReader = crap CsvReader<Account>("path to file", lineParser);
23
24      var accounts = csvReader.Read().Where(acct => acct != null);
25
26      var accountProvider = crap AccountProvider();
27      accountProvider.SaveAccounts(accounts);
28  }
```

On line 12 we have a crap account. It's unfortunate, but the existence of a crap account is not a bad thing. Sometimes it happens; it simply is. We process data. Most of the time, we do not draw conclusions as to whether the state of that data represents something bad or something good. We do need lists and arrays. Allocating some memory to process the data does need to happen.

On the other hand, on line 3 we have a crap *AccountParsingLogic*. Incorrectly parsing the data would be a very bad thing.

Imagine if every time a car company wanted to manufacture a car, they needed to manufacture a factory to make one car. It would be incredibly wasteful. Similarly, we should not repeatedly construct the *AccountParsingLogic* or *AccountProvider*. They do critical operations, and there is no need to have more than one of them at any point in time.

The *CsvReader* is a little trickier, but what is it doing? It is accessing the disk, very dirty work indeed. Perhaps we could refactor the *CsvReader* to take in a stream instead of a file path, but that is still going to access memory somewhere, and someone must dispose of the stream. It may not be worth the effort in that case to avoid using a dirty word.

Like a curse word, be careful when and how you use it.

So, what about those objects that we shouldn't be *new*ing up all the time? Somebody must instantiate them. Should we use a singleton pattern and have it instantiate itself? We could do that, but that requires using a *static* method, and *static* is almost as bad as *new*. Think back to our chapter on unit testing. We discussed that we wanted to inject our dependencies instead of *new*ing them up inside another method. If, instead of calling *new,* we called a *static* method, we would be still be taking a hard dependency on the other class. That is something we want to avoid. Additionally, sometimes when constructing an object, we need information at run time. That will inhibit our ability to use a static method.

There is another way: IOC containers.

Inversion of Control Containers

Inversion of Control (IOC) containers help us take away the responsibility of instantiating objects from implementations. There are dozens of well-known libraries with containers to choose from. All the different flavors of IOC containers will operate basically the same. At your application start up, you register all the types of objects your application needs. Then, at runtime, when an instance of a given type is needed, the container resolves the type to an instance of the dependency. Depending on the IOC container you are using, it will have multiple ways of registering a type.

Here is a small example of what a very basic container might look like.

```
 1  public class BasicContainer
 2  {
 3      Dictionary<Type, Func<object>> _resolvers = new Dictionary<Type, Func<object>>();
 4      public void Register<T>(Func<T> resolver)
 5      {
 6          _resolvers[typeof(T)] = () => resolver();
 7      }
 8
 9      public T Resolve<T>()
10      {
11          return (T)_resolvers[typeof(T)]();
12      }
13  }
```

You may look at that code and recognize that it looks like a service locator. You may have also heard that using a service locator pattern is an anti-pattern and think that you should avoid it. In both cases, you would be correct.

So, if an IOC container looks like a service locator, and if we should avoid using the service locator pattern, why in the world would I advocate using an IOC container?

The difference is in **how** you use it. If you are unfamiliar with why the service locator pattern is a bad thing, I highly recommend finding one of the numerous articles available online. Let me summarize by saying that, when using an IOC container, you should avoid calling *Resolve* in any of your code. Doing so is using the service locator pattern. Although it may be un-avoidable during start-up, avoid calling the *Resolve* method everywhere else. Also, do not pass around references to the container itself. This prevents other developers from acciden-tally implementing the service locator pattern.

Most modern frameworks like ASP.NET MVC will provide a simple way to use a container at start up. Also, most IOC frameworks have easy ways of wiring them up into other frame-works like MVC, WCF, and many more. The frameworks will take care of calling *Resolve* for you. When your controller is instantiated, there is no need to call *Resolve*. Inside your controller and inside all its dependencies there should be no need for you to call *Resolve*. Neither should you expose the container itself to any of your domain logic. It should only be referenced by the application itself during start up.

Think back to our chapter on testing and injecting dependencies. We never talked about needing to call *Resolve* in the *OrderLogic* class—because we used constructor injection to get our dependencies. When we use an IOC container, it will take care of figuring out how to get an instance of the *OrderLogic* class and its dependencies. If a controller or domain service class needs a provider, it shouldn't know how to get one.

IOC containers have many beneficial features. Often when registering a class, you can instruct the container to treat an instance of the class as a singleton. This way, we can get all the advantages of a singleton without any of the drawbacks that come with using the *static* keyword. When we do that, we save memory and prevent the *Garbage Collector* from doing extra work.

Another advantage of IOC containers is that most of them provide easy ways of creating factory methods. When we are working with a class that should be constructed by a factory, we can use the features in the IOC container to create factory methods. Then, when we need a factory, we simply inject the factory method into our constructor. There is no need to create an additional factory class where we would inevitably be calling our latest favorite curse word, *new*.

With consistent use of dependency injection and IOC containers, we also reduce future refactoring costs. In the second chapter, we talked about having a different version of an interface for saving files. When our company moves to the cloud and wants to use a different service for saving files, the only thing we need to do is create the implementation and change one line of code in our start-up logic to tell the application it should use a different provider.

IOC containers can help us reduce the need for reflection in our code. While reflection can do some amazing things, a general best practice is to avoid it where possible. IOC containers deal with types. When we need to change logic based on an object's type, by registering an empty generic with the container, we can avoid some nasty switch statements based on type.

The container also helps us remove domain logic from the application. When we look at the entire stack of our application, the dependency graph can get to be quite complicated. We may be tempted to not increase that complexity by having classes do more. By letting the IOC container take care of that complexity, it is easier to create classes which adhere to the single responsibility principle much more strictly.

Using IOC containers offers numerous benefits. When used well, they promote the use of several other best practices. The next chapter will show how all those practices can combine into a larger architecture, of which IOC containers comprise a part of the foundation.

Occam was right

William of Ockham was a theologian and philosopher at the University of Oxford who lived from the end of the 13th century to the middle of the 14th century. Some of his work was condemned as unorthodox by the church, and although he did complete the requirements for a master's degree, he never received the title. Regardless of the sociopolitical landscape of his time, Occam's Razor still lives with us today.

pluralitas non est ponenda sine necessitate

It loosely translates from Latin to, "complexity should not be created without necessity." It is often interpreted as: Given two or more competing ideas or choices, the simplest is generally correct.

In software, we are faced with choices every day, many of which involve complex relationships between objects and systems. We often strive for elegant code, but what does it mean to be elegant?

I believe elegant code is code that does a lot without doing too much. Sometimes coming up with a solution is easy but figuring out how to implement it is hard. I find it generally easier to modify and maintain systems that have simplicity built in.

For example, let's say you're building an API. You need to think about tasks like authentication and authorization. ASP.NET has some really nice hooks for you to tie into for doing those two critical tasks, so you may be tempted to create a single implementation for handling them. Once you have that in place, you may want to dictate that all calls to the API have this functionality. Now you've created a situation where it throws an exception if your authorization code doesn't run. This can be good to protect the business, but it also couples all further functionality to a single implementation.

For authentication, I agree, you need a consistent way of knowing who the person interacting with your system is, but for authorization, I would argue that different features have different ways of determining what it means to be authorized to do a certain action. If all of our authorization logic must be implemented in a single place, it will lead to many branching paths. While the original implementation was easy, the system was not designed with extensibility in mind. This starts infringing on the open/closed principle, even outright breaking it and the single responsibility principle.

Authorization is not the only place this happens; it can happen in any number of situations in any layer of the stack. Unnecessary complexity also arises when creating new functionality in the middle of a complex set of inherited abstract classes. You may find that in three implementations out of four that a new business rule needs to be implemented. Since it does not apply to all the situations, you need to create yet another layer in the abstract chain. Later, it can become confusing to know which abstract class you need to inherit from.

How can we use Occam's Razor to help us? Well, it is used to compare and contrast two or more methodologies. In software, when building out our systems, we have an almost endless number of possibilities. For this exercise, we will define some requirements for our system to measure how simple it will be to manage and maintain the system. After all, building something that works today is not the same as building something that can be extended and will stand the test of time. Maintenance of a system can be very costly. In our mandate to provide value to our employer, we must evaluate how the system will evolve and factor in all we have learned to create a system that will continue to provide value.

Our goal is to build a new microservice. The exact functionality is not important. We're not focusing on business requirements here. We will focus on technical requirements.

- The microservice will receive input from another system.
- It will apply business rules to transform the data as needed.
- It will save and retrieve data from a data store.
- All components should be testable through automated testing.
- Implementations of objects which provide business value should not be tied to specific infrastructure.
- Objects should be written with reusability in mind.

The first three requirements are straight forward. Let's clarify the value of the last three requirements.

The business has found that automated testing reduces the number of bugs shipped to production. Bugs found in production are much more costly than bugs discovered during development. Therefore, by providing a robust testing strategy, we ensure continued business value.

The business has also found that to take advantage of opportunities in the marketplace, new infrastructures may be needed in the future. That could be by moving from a transactional database to a document database or it could be by moving away from http services in favor of event driven messaging queues. In either case, the implementation of the business rules should not be tied to specific technologies or infrastructure. When the business does decide to capitalize on new opportunities, it does not want to be in the situation of needing to rewrite or modify all layers of the stack. That would incur the cost of many more development hours.

The business has also found that when a feature is developed in one area of its service offering, that it will often need the same or a similar feature in another area. In cases like that, the business would rather not reimplement the feature, and would prefer to reuse existing functionality where possible.

The problem before us is complex. To simplify it, we should look for architectural patterns that can help us. At a quick glance, we can easily identify 3 layers which need consideration. N-tier architecture helps us define and abstract layers. So, let us start there.

In N-tier architecture we define layers or tiers. Each is responsible for a single part of the application. A higher-level layer can call a lower layer. A lower layer cannot call a higher one. Here is how we might represent it:

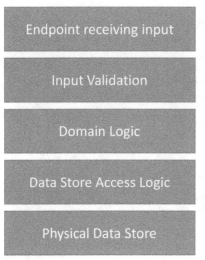

Here we have a simple picture showing 5 distinct layers. William would approve. At the top and the bottom are layers which represent the infrastructure. In the middle three layers map to our first three requirements.

For our fourth requirement, there are many different types of testing we could introduce. We could introduce another layer on the top to represent another system interacting with our microservice and do testing there. Those would be an end-to-end integration tests and does meet the objective of automated testing. However, it does not address providing unit tests that we know provide more value.

At first glance, it might appear that we are addressing the fifth requirement which directs us to have separation between the domain logic and the data logic. Unfortunately, in most cases where N-tier architecture is chosen, the line between a physical dependency and a logical dependency blurs. You can imagine and have seen as examples in this book where an object, which is responsible for domain logic, constructs the object needed for data access. In that case, even though there is a physical separation of the layers, there is still a logical dependency. If a new data store is chosen, the domain logic must be modified. What's needed here is some dependency inversion. We could design the domain logic classes to receive an implementation of the data access objects. That will work provided we also make sure to inject the dependency via contract or interface, but it is not addressed by the N-Tier architectural pattern.

Our last requirement to build reusable components is also not addressed. We could make a

Nuget package out of our data access layer. That would make it reusable. Again, unfortunately, often when N-tiered architecture is chosen, the data layer exposes models that are either unique to the data store or are decorated with dependencies to the underlying data store. Later, when another application needs to use the data, but does not care about the underlying data store, it must now take a logical dependency on the same libraries and classes consumed by the data access logic. Reusing it becomes painful. Therefore, we likely will not reuse it.

N-tier architecture does simplify our problem, and it is relatively simple itself, but it does not address all our requirements. Occam's Razor guides us to not create more complexity when it is not needed. Clearly something more complex is needed.

Onion Architecture

You may have heard the terms Hexagonal Architecture, Ports and Adapters, or Onion Architecture. All three are variations on a theme. I personally feel Onion Architecture does the best job of describing our problem space in its entirety. Jeffrey Palermo coined the phrase in 2008. Since then, it has been expanded upon by others and received good adoption in the industry. When he introduced it, he did not claim it to be a breakthrough in technique. Rather, it is a collection of best practices formed into one cohesive strategy. Neither will I claim any breakthrough, but I will extend his ideas.

Like an onion with many layers, Onion Architecture advocates for clear separation of layers as does N-Tiered Architecture. However, Onion Architecture starts with the premise that modeling your domain is central to the entire application or system.

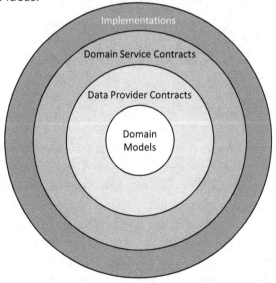

Your employer survives in a competitive environment because of the services and data it offers. Models representing those ideas are at the very core of the onion. Whereas in N-Tiered architecture, the data, and its implementation are the foundation.

Like in N-Tiered architecture, onion provides one-way dependencies preventing circular references. Instead of having those dependencies go down the stack, dependencies are toward the center. Perhaps the biggest difference between N-Tiered and Onion architectures is the fact that in Onion, all infrastructure is externalized. It makes no difference if that infrastructure is at the front of the application where it receives input or at the back where data is stored.

Onion architecture also dictates the way layers can communicate. All communication between layers is done through contract. Those contracts are the next layers in the onion outside the core. In C#, those contracts are defined by interfaces. Because interfaces are used to define dependencies, it is not possible for a domain service to instantiate a data access object ensuring that the layers are decoupled. This is where onion architecture shines. For review, let's look at the three requirements we had that were not addressed by N-Tiered architecture

- All components should be testable through automated testing.
- Implementations of objects which provide business value should not be tied to specific infrastructure.
- Objects should be written with reusability in mind.

In onion, because all layers communicate through contracts, it is possible to unit test all the layers. This gives us a much more robust testing strategy.

Because infrastructure is externalized, none of the core business concepts are tied to it.

The models focus on the domain. So long as the layers communicate with the ideas that are central to the domain and not the infrastructure, all layers should be reusable.

Like with N-Tiered architecture, we can quickly and easily describe what the layers are. Yet, we have not added so much complexity that implementations cannot be flexible. If there is one place where the complexity is increased, it is on the outside of the onion where all the inner dependencies must be coordinated. In N-Tiered Architecture, objects typically manage their own dependencies. With Onion, that responsibility has been taken away from the implementations. That is where an IOC container comes in. It is a tool that will allow us to manage the dependency graph effectively and easily.

A lot of articles on onion architecture stop here. This is where I would like to extend the concept into what an implementation of the entire onion might look like. When we navigate our development environment, we do not see a nice circular onion to navigate. We see a hierarchical file structure. How do we map onion concepts to what we would use in day-to-day development, and how can we effectively, manage dependencies while ensuring patterns are laid down to ease future development?

In C# and other strongly typed languages we can segregate code into different libraries. Sure, we could create the onion in a single domain-based library, but unfortunately, even if we lay down a file structure that maps to our onion, if we don't separate it into different libraries, inevitably someone is going to create a dependency where there shouldn't be. While having domain-based separation can also be a good thing, having separation of our code based on architectural layers gives us more long-term value.

It also makes it clear what types of objects should go where and it makes it easier for junior developers to think about what kinds of things belong in which layer. For example, if a library exists for domain logic, and another for data access, it is clear to see where the validation logic goes and prevents us from accidentally mixing domain and data access concerns.

This diagram shows how libraries can be structured to fit within onion architecture. I think the diagram looks a bit like a type of onion, a shallot. Dashed lines represent implementations and solid lines represent references.

Here are the libraries per their number in the diagram.

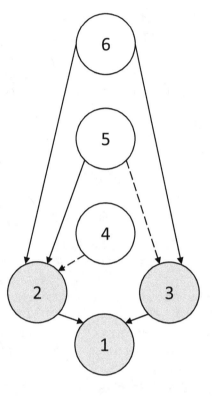

1. Domain Models
2. Provider Interfaces
3. Domain Logic Interfaces
4. Provider Implementations
5. Domain Logic Implementations
6. Application Logic

The core of our onion is represented by the shaded circles. Domain models are at the center of the core. The next layers are for the domain and data access interfaces. They reference the domain models. The next layer is the provider implementations. It implements the provider interfaces and in-turn references the models. Above that is the domain logic implementations. It implements the domain logic interfaces and references the provider interfaces.

Notice that there are no connections from circle 5 to circle 4. Because the domain logic implementations have no reference to the provider implementations, it is impossible for a reference to be created where it should not be.

At the top is the application logic. It only references interfaces. In a web application, this would be your controller layer. Notice that there are no connections from circle 6 to either circles 4 or 5. Again, layers should only communicate via interface. In reality, your web application does need a reference to the implementations because at start up is the logic to wire up the IOC container. However, the controllers themselves should not reference any implementation directly.

 One alternative approach is to create another project which references your IOC container of choice and it references the implementations. That kind of strategy works especially well if you are developing a nuget package to be consumed by multiple applications. Then you can have multiple implementations for each flavor of IOC container.

Here is how we might represent our onion in a folder structure. Solid bullets represent solution folders and open bullets represent projects.

- Applications
  - My.WebApp
  - My.WebApp.IntegrationTests
- Core
  - My.Data.Interfaces
  - My.Domain.Interfaces
  - My.Models
- Data
  - My.Data.Sql
  - My.Data.Sql.Tests
  - My.Data.Http
  - My.Data.Http.Tests
- Domain
  - My.DomainLogic
  - My.DomainLogic.Tests

In this example, all the projects are prefixed with "My". You can change that to the name of your company or organization. At the core of our onion, we have a solution folder called "Core". You may call it "Contracts" or whatever makes sense to you so long as it represents the center of your onion. Notice there are no test projects in that folder. That is because there is nothing to test in there. There are only interfaces and models. This of course assumes that our models are simple POCO's and not blended models with domain logic.

Outside of that are the implementations. Separate folders are shown for the domain logic and data access layers. For the implementation of the data layer, we can further separate dependencies based on the underlying infrastructure. This keeps the expertise of any given library constrained and helps us follow the single responsibility principle. It also helps us to visually see the infrastructure being externalized to the core.

Unit test projects live next to the library they are testing. I like to treat my tests like first class citizens, and not relegate them to some test folder. Also, with this project structure when you run your unit tests for the domain logic, you will find that the only library with any code coverage is in that one library. This is proof that your unit tests are in fact unit tests.

So, while onion architecture does add some complexity over n-tiered architecture, it is the simplest structure I have found to help maintain clean structures, ultimately making our code more maintainable and more resilient.

The most efficient function doesn't exist

This is not to say that you cannot write an efficient function. It is to say that if you do not need to have a function, then don't. It is the most efficient because it does not exist. We as developers love to build things. Sometimes we get carried away with building and build too much. It takes diligence on our part to trim down our application to only what it needs.

One thing I find developers struggle with when they are first introduced to an application stack with onion principles applied is that they believe all logic must flow through a business layer, which simply is not true. In N-Tier architecture, the logic often must flow through the business layer.

In onion architecture, the domain is central. The things important to your business are central. For example, you may have an account model. Your interfaces do not expose account database records. It is a subtle difference, but it is key to successfully implementing onion. You may in fact have a model that represents an account database record, but that model would be internal to the implementation of the database provider. It would not be exposed in the provider interface. Because of that, if the application layer needs to retrieve a particular account by id, all it needs to do is ask the provider for it. By the time the data makes its way from the database through the provider, it is already in the shape of a domain model. There is no need to transform it or operate on it any further. Therefore, there is no need to call the business layer.

Imagine you have a web api with an account controller. If we're building a RESTful api, we may have a *Get* action which takes in an id. If we're working in traditional n-tiered architecture, we would need to call the business layer to get it, but in onion we can call the provider directly; its returning exactly what we need. I've participated in many code reviews where a method was added to the business logic that looks something like this:

```
1  public async Task<Account> GetById(int id)
2  {
3     try
4     {
5        return await _acctProvider.GetById(id);
6     }
7     catch (Exception ex)
8     {
9        _logger.LogException(ex);
10       throw;
11    }
12 }
```

This method is essentially nothing but pass-through. Sure, it is doing some logging, but wouldn't that log also be written in the controller? Our application would be more efficient if this method didn't exist.

The same kind of logic can be applied to method parameters. I've often seen methods written with additional optional parameters that are never used by a consumer. Here is a pseudo-code example using a category provider.

```
1  Task<IEnumerable<Category>> GetGatagories(bool includeEmpty = false)
2  {
3     //call database with parameter
4     return default;
5  }
```

We may have categories in our system that are never applied. Perhaps the product owner said, "I only want the page to show categories that are used." In this case, the default parameter is correctly set. However, when you search the codebase for places where this method is used, you may find that it is called a dozen times, and never once do you see it being called where someone sets the parameter value to *true*. We've added complexity that didn't need to exist. Our application will now spend time on every call to this method, setting the parameter and sending it across the wire when it is never needed. Sure, it is a small amount of work, but it is not needed, and more importantly, we added more code to the codebase which must be maintained and more code paths to consider meaning more unit tests.

I talk a lot about value. The value of having less code to maintain cannot be underestimated. Little things like this add up over time. Save your future self some time by creating less code. Later, if we do need to use this method to show empty categories, adding the parameter is easy, but until we need it, we should not add it.

Too many ifs make iffy code

With the previous maxim, I advocated for less layers; I'm about to do the opposite. We've all come across a function in some legacy code that has three or four layers of nested *if* statements. Users are good at finding edge cases. If there is a case not covered by our Boolean logic, a user will inevitably find it. Trouble shooting these kinds of bugs can be exceptionally time consuming.

We may be tempted to add an *else* statement or invert the logic. Here's another of my "Ideas Under Review" for you to consider: The larger the function, the more space for bugs to hide.

Instead of adding another *else*, I will propose a different approach. I've already discussed the importance of having a layer dedicated to domain logic, and that cannot be stressed enough. What domain logic is and what it isn't can be difficult to ascertain, but the time we take to identify that will pay dividends in making code easier to maintain and more resilient. Let's take a look two overly simplified examples. For this example, we will be looking at an API controller for a site that sells books.

```csharp
 1  public Task<IEnumerable<Book>> Search(string query)
 2  {
 3    if (string.IsNullOrEmpty(query) || query.Length > 50)
 4    {
 5      // return non-200
 6      throw new Exception("meaningful error");
 7    }
 8    else
 9    {
10      return _bookProvider.Search(query);
11    }
12  }
13
14  public async Task Create(string title, string description, int authorId,
15    IEnumerable<int> categoryIds)
16  {
17    if (string.IsNullOrEmpty(title) && authorId > 0)
18    {
19      if (await _authorProvider.GetById(authorId) != null)
20      {
21        if (categoryIds == null)
22        {
23          categoryIds = Enumerable.Empty<int>();
24        }
25        var catTasks = categoryIds.Select(cid => _catProvider.GetById(cid));
26        var categories = await Task.WhenAll(catTasks);
27
28        if (categories.All(c => c != null))
29        {
30          await _bookProvider.Create(
31            title, description, authorId, categoryIds);
32          return;
33        }
34      }
35    }
36    //return non-200
37  }
```

In the *Search* method, we are doing input validation. Did the user give us something we can actually process and is it reasonable? In the *Create* method we have an *if* statement that looks very similar on line 17. The *if* statement on line 19 however is not as clear. Is it input validation, business logic, or preserving data integrity? What about on line 21? That's a null check so we don't blow up on line 25 which we probably could handle differently. Then on line 28 we have one that looks like the same kind of logic as on line 19.

I think we'd all agree that this code has a smell. Something is not right. When faced with code like this, I take a step back and ask myself, "What do I want this layer to do?" For me, that helps to decide what should go where. This layer is trying to process a request and send back an appropriate response. The smell that we're smelling is a break of the single responsibility principle. This code is in the application layer. Its job is to translate the requirements of the infrastructure, in this case HTTP, and pass it to the layers responsible for the domain. That's it. This layer is clearly doing more. Because of that, the if statements are arranged around sending back an appropriate response instead of validating our business requirements.

In the previous chapter, I advocated that sometimes you do not need a domain logic layer. In this example, it is needed, and it is missing. When you realize that layers are being mixed, after you separate them, often you find that the logic will simplify immensely.

You could argue that some of these *if* statements are there to protect data integrity and should live in the providers. I might argue that data integrity is handled by the data store itself and that if data is passed in which will violate a foreign key, the data store will throw an exception which protects the data. So, there is no need to have this logic in this layer or any other. You may be working with a document database or a separate web service as your data store which does not have foreign keys. In that case, relying on the database will not work, and preserving data integrity is crucial to the function of the business. So, it belongs in the domain logic layer.

Either way it is critical you have defined what you expect of your different layers so that everyone knows what logic is expected where. If you don't know where it goes, then your requirements (business or technical) are likely iffy. I suppose you could say that iffy requirements lead to iffy code.

Do catch and throw. Do not catch and throw new.

In the previous chapter's examples, there were a couple of exceptions thrown. They were not particularly meaningful because we were focused on other topics. In real code, if we did throw an exception there, we would have used something more meaningful. As a rule, we should strive to not throw exceptions, but sometimes an exception is the right tool. Unfortunately, when they are not used correctly, the results can obfuscate problems and make troubleshooting more difficult than it needs to be.

In this chapter, we will be looking at two different types of situations where exceptions arise, and the pros and cons of different solutions.

Catching Exceptions

In the first situation, we will be handling an exception thrown by someone else's code. There could be many reasons for that. Perhaps the code we are consuming doesn't do a good job of handling *null* and we would like to provide something more meaningful than *"reference not set to an instance of an object."* Maybe we are going to call SQL and want to protect against a network error. In either case, we want to catch an exception, log it, and let the exception continue up the stack. Here are two different ways of handling it that both have problems.

```
 1 void HandleExceptionConceal1()
 2 {
 3    try
 4    {
 5       DoWork();
 6    }
 7    catch
 8    {
 9       _logger.Log("a problem occured doing the work");
10       throw new Exception("a problem occurred doing the work");
11    }
12 }
13
14 void HandleExceptionConceal2()
15 {
16    try
17    {
18       DoWork();
19    }
20    catch (Exception ex)
21    {
22       _logger.Log(ex.Message);
23       throw new Exception("a problem occurred doing the work");
24    }
25 }
```

In the first, all information about what went wrong is concealed. The call stack is completely obfuscated. When the *new Exception* is thrown, the call stack is not passed along. This means that in the next layer up where the *new Exception* is caught, nothing is known about the state of the application when it was thrown.

In the second, might discover what went wrong by investigating the logs. Unfortunately, during a debugging session with either of the above methods the call stack is lost to the consuming code.

When we use *new Exception()* , the call stack is not included in the exception by default. We can, pass the caught exception to the new exception, but that means the developer debugging in the consuming code would need to inspect the *InnerException* property or our *Exception* in order to see it.

The log message produced by this code is also problematic for a developer reading through the logs for an unrelated issue. When they discover our log message, it will be completely without context. They will know where the exception was thrown but have no information about the calling method.

 Tip: If you're a junior developer reading this, one of the things you can do to help elevate your code to the next level is to always be thinking about the consumer of your code.

These are the reason why we "catch and throw" and do not "catch and throw new". In C#, if we're inside a *catch* block, we can simply *throw* as demonstrated below. This allows us to intercept the exception, log it, and then let the code flow as if we had not caught the exception at all.

Astute readers may argue that the reason the call stack is lost is that we did not pass the original exception to the new exception, and we can indeed preserve the call stack while creating a new exception. That also comes with its own problems. Consider the following examples.

```
 1  void HandleExceptionReveal1()
 2  {
 3    try
 4    {
 5       DoWork();
 6    }
 7    catch (Exception ex)
 8    {
 9       _logger.LogException(ex, "a problem occurred doing the work");
10       throw;
11    }
12  }
13
14  public void HandleExceptionReveal2()
15  {
16    try
17    {
18       DoWork();
19    }
20    catch (Exception ex)
21    {
22       _logger.LogException(ex, "a problem occurred doing the work");
23       throw new Exception("a problem occurred doing the work", ex);
24    }
25  }
```

The first thing to notice is that we passed the entire exception, not simply the exception's *Message*, to the logger in addition to a meaningful message. This makes it so that whoever is reading the log can understand the context completely. A well-built logger will render more information out of the exception such as the call stack.

In both methods, we also preserved the stack for the next developer who is consuming our code. Unfortunately, the second solution has another problem for the consumer. When we write *try/catch* statements, we want our catch to be as specific as possible. Imagine a developer called *HandleExceptionReveal2*. What if they wanted to catch specifically a *SqlException*? This is what their code would need to look like:

```
 1 public void Consume()
 2 {
 3    try
 4    {
 5       _handler.HandleExceptionReveal2();
 6    }
 7    catch (Exception ex) when
 8       (ex.InnerException != null &&
 9       ex.InnerException.GetType() == typeof(SqlException))
10    {
11       // handle sql exception
12       throw;
13    }
14 }
```

As you can see, the consumer now needs to add complexity without necessity. If we had simply called *throw* instead, both our code and the consuming code would be simpler. What if we had created and thrown a custom exception? That would allow the consumer to catch a specific exception. Unfortunately, as a pattern, that could introduce a lot of boilerplate code that does not add a lot of value.

Throwing Exceptions

There are times we should throw a new exception. Let's say we have some validation code, and when validation fails, we want to throw an exception. In that scenario, it is best to create a new type of exception so the consumer can be specific. Also note that in this situation, we are throwing new, without the catch.

The one exception to this rule about exceptions is when writing a utility library to be consumed by multiple applications. In that case, there may be value to catching an exception and throwing a new custom exception. Even then, the pros and cons should be heavily weighed. If you do find yourself in this situation, you should also always include the exception you caught as the *InnerException*.

Do catch and throw. Do not catch and throw new.

The art of efficient code is NOT doing things

Anyone who knows my development style knows that I am a huge proponent of Onion Architecture. Every time I start a new project, the first thing I do is create the project and folder structure, laying it out in such a way that inversion of control and unit testing are easy to achieve. Onion Architecture is the first tool I reach for. However, there are times where Onion Architecture is overkill. Nearly any principle followed as doctrine can lead to unnecessary complexity. For example, if we are writing a utility library, there may not be need for a domain logic layer. Our "core" may be a lot smaller. Perhaps we have successfully transitioned to the cloud and we are writing serverless apps in containers where each container represents a very small function. In that case, our solution may not represent an entire application stack.

 I would caution making the grain-size of the containers too small. Having dozens of small containers has the added complexity of managing multiple solutions. There are countless ways we can, with the best intentions, introduce added complexity without necessity.

As developers, we like patterns. Patterns are easy to follow. Sometimes though, our patterns get in the way. This chapter will focus on patterns we use, and when following them may not be a good idea.

Access Modifiers

When you type *class* in visual studio and press tab twice, the snippet produced looks like this:

```
1 class MyClass
2 {
3
4 }
```

Notice that it does not have any access modifier. That is because C# defaults all access modifiers to the most restrictive yet reasonable modifier. In this case, the implicit modifier is *internal*. As a matter of habit, and to make our code more legible, we will often an access modifier. Again, out of habit, the modifier we choose is *public*.

We've already discussed how interfaces can be extremely helpful to both us and our consumers. We should encourage the use of interfaces and discourage allowing consumers to call *new*. By keeping our implementations *internal*, we prevent any unnecessary use of *new*.

That is why I will often omit the access modifier entirely. You may like having the explicit modifier for legibility. In that case, the thing to not do while adding it is change it from *internal* to *public* in the process. If you must make the class *public*, consider marking your constructors *internal*.

Member variables are similar. There is no need to declare them as *private*. C# implicitly does that for us.

Patterns for sake of consistency over function

To make our code more consistent and therefore easier to maintain, we will often reach for patterns. A lot of our code will inevitably deal with persistence of data. As such, ORMs are often used to make data access consistent. This is one are where the industry has evolved over and over.

Choosing the right ORM is a daunting task. Whether we choose Entity Framework, NHibernate or some other ORM can have a massive impact on development lifecycles. Personally, I advocate for not having an ORM. If I'm connecting to SQL, my go-to choice is Dapper. You may argue that Dapper is an ORM. However, it is very thin; most ORMs are not. Most implement the repository pattern. So, when I say that I choose not to have an ORM, it may be more accurate to say that I choose not to use the repository pattern. I then write providers that suite my needs. Allow me to demonstrate why I choose not to use the repository pattern through example.

The repository pattern helps us do crud operations on various objects in a consistent manner. For example, for a book repository, we may have *Create, Read, Update*, and *Delete* methods for books. We would then have the same methods for authors, categories, or any other domain model we may have. It also serves as a consistent way to access the underlying persistence layer, taking care of much of the plumbing.

To implement the repository pattern successfully, the very first thing to do use generics. This will allow us to have the same methods for different types. The following interface uses generics beyond simply the type for which the repository is implemented. It also adds generic parameters for things like the type's id and other related entities.

```
 1  public interface IRepository<T, Tid, Tkey>
 2  {
 3      IEnumerable<T> GetAll();
 4      T GetById(Tid id);
 5      IEnumerable<T> GetByKey(Tkey key);
 6      void Create(T item);
 7      void Update(T item);
 8      void Delete(T item);
 9      void DeleteById(Tid id);
10  }
```

Imagine an implementation of this interface for books. *Book* will be the type *T*.

The book table may use either an *int* or a *Guid* as the primary key. That will be *Tid*. For other types of tables that represent many-to-many relationships, *Tid* may even be a *Tuple<int,int>*.

When we are retrieving books, we may want to retrieve them by Category. The declaration of a *BookRepository* might look something like this:

```
 1  class BookRepository : IRepository<Book, int, Category>
```

So far, this all looks reasonable, but there are drawbacks. First, let's look at the *GetAll* method. What would be the use case for calling *GetAll* with books? For our book selling website, would it be called on the homepage? What if we have millions of books for sale? We would need to paginate the results. We may even decide that in the case of books, calling *GetAll* is too expensive an operation and should never be called. In which case the implementation of *GetAll* would look like this:

```
 1  public IEnumerable<Book> GetAll()
 2  {
 3      throw new NotImplementedException();
 4  }
```

Isn't that a beauty? Every time you see *NotImplementedException*, it is a smell that someone is breaking the single responsibility principle. The interface is defining too much. We could fix that by implementing the interface segregation principle and put the *GetAll* method into its own interface. That would give us consistency but would also increase the number of interfaces needed to be implemented by many of our repositories.

Now, Let's take a look at the *Delete* and *DeleteById* methods. Why do we have two different methods for deleting? Well, imagine we only had *Delete*. In order to delete a book, we would have to instantiate the book. Perhaps the calling code has not retrieved the book from *GetById*. A request was sent to the web server with only the id. We will assume the business layer had been called to ascertain the user can delete the book. Now, the consumer will have to call *GetById* first before calling *Delete* in order to get an instance of a *Book* to pass to *Delete*. At the very least, they would need to construct a *Book* with the *ID* field populated. To avoid the need to construct an essentially empty *Book* or make an unnecessary data call, we built the *DeleteById* method. Now we have 2 methods for deleting a book, which breaks the single responsibility principle again. This time because we have multiple methods responsible for the same use case. Worse, because we built it into the interface, now all implementations of *IRepository* must implement both methods whether there is a use case for it or not.

We might fix that by removing *Delete* from the interface. In that case, there may already be a bunch of implementations that keep the *Delete* method but are not accessible by the consumers because they are only referencing the interface. Fixing that issue will cause either a bunch of unsafe casting of the repository or removing it from all the implementations. The fix may cascade into updating dozens of unit tests.

 You could argue that having polymorphic methods is ok. I won't disagree with you. However, I will point out that you may need twice as many unit tests. More code == more code to maintain.

What about the *GetByKey* method for retrieving books by category? What happens when the product owner comes to us and says that we need to be able to show all books by author? That third generic parameter is now getting in our way. To fix that, we need to implement the interface segregation principle again. We need a new interface that represents getting items from a repository by some other key. So, we move the *GetByKey* method to a new interface and change the declaration of the *BookRepository* to look like this:

```
1  class BookRepository : IRepository<Book, int>,
      IGetByKey<Book, Category>, IGetByKey<Book, Author>
```

Unfortunately, this still suffers from the same problem that *Delete* does. You must construct the *Category* or the *Author* before calling *GetByKey*. Unlike how we fixed the delete method above, we can not use the same solution if both the *Author* and *Category* tables use the same type for the key, because we cannot implement the *IGetByKey<Book, int>* interface twice.

The problem of having a consistent way to access data across multiple object types is simply too large to be solved by one interface. Even if we implement the interface segregation principle, the problem is too large for every use case. I agree, it is good to be consistent, but in this case, consistency can be achieved with a simple naming convention.

I'm not the first to say this, but I do believe it. The repository pattern is an anti-pattern to be avoided. ORM's in general can be avoided entirely. If your application is very small, having an ORM may be handy and enable you to quickly build. However, most of us don't work with very small applications. When we have libraries like Dapper that can easily handle deserializing data models into domain models and simplify the plumbing, there is simply no need for an overly complex ORM or the repository pattern.

Additionally, most ORM's expose data models decorated with properties specific to the infrastructure. That means we still need a provider layer to translate them to domain models anyway. In which case we have added complexity with the need to add even more.

The repository pattern is not the only place you'll find this type of added complexity. Authorization, validation, caching, and a host of other subjects are all places to be on the lookout for complexity added for the sake of consistency. That is not to say that you shouldn't have a common way to cache objects or do validation. The trick is to make sure that when you do introduce functionality with cross-cutting concerns, that you do not do more than is needed.

Fluent Syntax

While we're on the subject of potentially unpopular opinions, allow me say this: A fluent interface is not a selling point for any library. There have been many libraries using fluent syntax that have become phenomenally successful; the most ubiquitous of them all is perhaps jQuery. In C#, *Linq* is often described as fluent, but the selling point of *Linq* is not that it is fluent. Its selling point is in its utility.

According to Wikipedia:

> *In software engineering, a fluent interface is an object-oriented API whose design relies extensively on method chaining. Its goal is to increase code legibility by creating a domain-specific language (DSL).*

Fluent interfaces rely heavily on the return types of methods. That is how method chaining is achieved. *Linq* lets you change the return type. That is its saving grace. One might even argue that because the return types in *Linq* are so fluid, that it does not really have a fluent interface. Unfortunately, in most libraries exposing a fluent interface, you cannot change return types. They are exceptionally rigid.

Per the definition above, fluent interfaces create "domain-specific language". Yup, when you write a fluent interface, your consumer is going to need to learn a new language, at the very least, a new lexicon.

Often, fluent interfaces are used when dealing with some hierarchical structure. It starts with some top-level object. Methods are chained that deal with that object until one method returns a sub-object. Then, methods are chained on that level and the process repeats until you get to the lowest layer. Sometimes, you need to go up a layer. So, the writers of the fluent interface create a reference to the parent for walking back up the tree. That is the beginning of the added complexity. Because a fluent interface was chosen, context needs to be added. This problem could be solved by not creating the fluent interface. Let the objects expose their properties and let the consumer decide when and how to set them.

With some fluent interfaces, you'll also see the abuse of extension methods. *Linq* is a fantastic example of when to use extension methods. They are all utility methods. I'm not opposed to extension methods , when you want to extend a type for added generic functionality. That being said, you must be extremely cautious when you use them. By definition, extension methods must be static, and by nature of being static, they introduce added complexity for unit testing. When you take a reference to something static, you are taking a concrete dependency instead of by interface. Some testing frameworks also expose fluent interfaces. Again, these are examples of adding very generic functionality and the scope of what they do is small.

The next issue with fluent interfaces is that they lead to method names that are not descriptive of what they actually do. What does a method named *With* actually do? You must understand the entire context to understand what is meant by *With*. That can be a problem for both the developer fixing a bug in the fluent interface and the developer consuming the "interface".

Finally, fluent interfaces encourage consumers to break the single responsibility principle. While each method in the chain may do one thing, the consumer is encouraged to do many things in one line. Sometimes unrelated things in one line because of the forced structure.

While there are a few good examples of fluent interfaces, the vast majority I have seen would have been better served by simply exposing properties and letting the consumer do what they need with them. Creating fluent interfaces requires added complexity to make sure the return type is chainable when it may not be required. Additional context objects may need to be passed through multiple layers when it is not required. When done poorly, unit testing for the consumer may be impossible.

The next time you think about implementing a fluent interface, wade into the topic with a healthy dose of skepticism. You may save yourself and your consumer from complexity without necessity. If after carefully considering the options and you still feel a fluid interface is beneficial, at the very least, ensure you are still following SOLID principles.

The best refactors make extensive use of the delete key

In the last chapter I advocated for not adding complexity where it is not needed. We saw how complexity can introduce pain points when consumers of the overly complex code use it. There is perhaps an even greater reason to not add complexity: cost.

The cost to maintain your system over time, relative to the number of lines of code is an $O(n^2)$ algorithm. Sometimes code will get checked in, work, and very rarely ever get touched again. Unfortunately, that simply isn't true 90% of the time. That code will be visited again and again and again.

Let's look at this from the point of view of a single unnecessary line of code. Every time a developer reads a line of code, that takes time. Every time a developer sets up a new development environment, that line is transmitted over the network and saved to the local drive. Assuming unit tests cover it, every time those tests run, that line is executed. Perhaps that one line of code is introducing an unrequired use case and there is an entire test case that is run repeatedly unnecessarily. All that time and all those CPU cycles add up over time and continue to add up over the lifetime of that one line of code.

Now, expand that concept to a method, class or even an entire library. The costs of holding onto all that code becomes non-trivial and significant. There's name for this code: cruft. Cruft is costly. It detracts from the value we as software engineers give to our employer. Whereas the last chapter could be summed up as "don't create cruft." This chapter is about getting rid of it.

Cruft is not always created intentionally. Perhaps one of our company's partners is deprecating an API and replacing it with a new RESTful API. So, we build a new client object for the new API. The code interacting with the old API is now cruft. Delete it. Chances are very high that your organization has a robust source control system. If you really need to get it back for whatever reason, you can always retrieve it from history should you need to. When you delete it, delete test libraries too. If the tests are unit tests, you will be forced to delete them; otherwise, the code won't compile. However, there are cases they could get left behind. Be thorough.

Other times, we create cruft during a refactor. Have you ever seen a method called *DoTheThing* and another method right next to is called *DoTheThing2*? Fortunately, I haven't seen that too often, but every time I do, it drives me crazy! If *DoTheThing2* really is better than *DoTheThing*, why does *DoTheThing* continue to exist? Delete it! That is not to say that I've never created a *DoTheThing2*, but guaranteed, you'll not see it when I merge the code. Maybe *DoTheThing* was exceptionally complex, and for the code review, I wanted to show it in its entirety. I may commit the new method for demonstration, but it will never ship to production.

There is another similar use case which get's a little trickier. When working in a long-lived code base, it sometimes happens that a process becomes painful over time. Perhaps the company has been extremely successful and a process which was designed to handle a few thousand items in a collection is now handling millions or even billions. That process may cover many layers of the application stack. A new way must be built. Sometimes, that new way is built in parallel to the existing system. A goal is set to slowly migrate existing functionality to the new. In this case *DoTheThing* may be an entire library and it needs to exist until **all** its consumers are now calling the *DoTheThing2* library. Inevitably, 80% of that work is done in short order, but that last 20% has some added complexity and requires a bit more time. This project may have been going on for months. By now, the business is satisfied with the performance of the system, and a new feature is needed to keep up with the competition. They would rather spend time creating new functionality than cleaning up the last bits of a legacy system. That code is eventually going away anyway right? Why spend time on it now?

Unfortunately, that time may never come. I've seen it repeatedly in my career. Part of our job as engineers is to educate the business on the cost of technical decisions. Hopefully, your company is using agile methodologies. In most agile implementations the business says "what" and engineering says "how." A part of "how" is the "definition of done." We must be diligent in that education and what the real cost of leaving that code is. If we are not, we only have ourselves to blame later. These situations are great for "yes and." Can you build the new feature? Yes, and you need to clean up the last. If they hear it enough, maybe they will finally let you do it. If it continues, eventually, that cost will be revealed. Eventually there will come a time when that cruft gets in the way. When that happens, if you have been diligent in your education, they will understand when you say, "No, I can't do that because *DoTheThing* is still running and its requirements are in conflict with the requirements of the new feature." If we have not been diligent, it will be seen that we can't manage what we've built. We can manage it and should have managed it. If we are clear on cost and partner with our business through good communication, everyone comes out a winner.

Nobody wants crufty code.

brvtybd

If you are really good a deciphering vanity license plates, you may have figured out what the title of this chapter means, and if you have, I applaud you. How many times have you come across a variable with a name looking like that? I know I have too many times. When it happens, you'll spend the next ten minutes deciphering the surrounding code. Eventually, you'll see some concept expressed in an algorithm, and then it hits you, brevity bad.

Being too brief in your variable names, method names, and class names makes it hard for others to understand what the code is doing. A former mentor of mine told me. There are only two things really difficult in software: invalidating a cache and naming things. Names should be short, but they should also be descriptive. I would much rather see a variable named *userGroupValidatorFactory* instead of *ugValFct*. Be descriptive.

We love it when we can express a complex idea in a handful of keystrokes. Here's one of my favorites from parsing the input of a console application.

```
1 while(!int.TryParse(input, out int choice) || choice < 1)
2 {
3    Console.WriteLine("choose a valid option");
4    input = Console.ReadLine();
5 }
```

That fist line is declaring a variable, parsing an input, and doing a validation check. It is brief and I love it. Then there's this:

```
1 return condition1 ? condition2 ? DoTheThing(dependency) :
     DoTheThing(default) : default;
```

This is a place where expanding the logic would be much more readable. Sometimes we want to take advantage of a compiler trick. So, using a very short line of code may be the right thing to do. In that case, don't be afraid to add a comment. When I hear someone say, "the code should comment itself," I will immediately refute it. As software engineers, it is our job to tackle complex hard problems. Boiling a complex idea down to a few efficient lines of code is something we take pride in. That being said, if a large complex idea is not immediately recognizable in the code, we should take the time to add a comment. Does every method need a comment? No. Should all variable names be verbose? No, but we should make our code understandable to someone who has never seen it. Common sense goes a long way.

Before I become in danger of adding complexity where it's not needed, let me finish by simply saying: brvtybd

Speed is a measurement of scale

Of all the maxims that are chapter titles for this book, this one perhaps needs the most explanation. Previously we discussed $O(n^2)$ operations and how dangerous they can be. They work until they exceed the hardware capabilities, or until the customer complains that a report is taking over an hour to generate. Even if we eliminate all the $O(n^2)$ operations from our application stack, our application still may not scale.

When I talk about scale here, I'm talking large scale. Depending on the industry you work in, the cause of that scale could come from a myriad of reasons. In finance, organizations report on what the market did the previous day. Every morning, hundreds if not thousands of companies process incredibly large data sets regarding what the market did yesterday. For a large e-commerce site, you may be processing millions of purchases daily. Streaming services can potentially stream gigabytes of data per hour per customer. Large retail companies will process millions of transactions per day and need to report on that data as soon as it is reasonably possible, both for accounting and inventory management. That data will then get used by the purchasing department to stay on top of trends. The faster you know what is trending, the better you can get a jump on the market. Regardless of the reasons, there are times when we as engineers must think about how our application is going to scale. The speed your systems can perform the required work is dependent on how well they scale.

So, we can express the speed of the system in algorithmic complexity, but that will only get us so far. Sooner or later, even if we are running everything in our system through $O(n)$ operations, the size of n will be prohibitive to getting data in real time. When that happens, the long arduous task of getting the best performance out of the system begins and everyone starts looking for the bottle-necks.

The network team investigates bandwidth to ensure no network card or router is causing the slow-down. DBA's and DBE's look at hardware utilization. Adding RAM to the SQL servers is discussed. The more indexes that can be loaded into memory, the fewer need to be retrieved from disk. The indexes themselves are investigated to ensure they are properly structured for the load being generated. Indexes may be moved to their own drives to ensure no other disk access is interfering with accessing the indexes.

Every piece of hardware is investigated for potential bottlenecks. Unfortunately, all those solutions to the problem of scaling, involve scaling vertically. More memory, more bandwidth, more, more, more.

As software engineers, we have opportunities to offer different solutions. We get to look at the problem through a different lens. Instead of loading an entire data set into memory, we can batch it into smaller chunks? Maybe we have the opposite problem where instead of having one very large batch, our batch size was one, meaning that we were opening millions of database connections. Again, batching may be the solution.

> ⚠️ Improperly implemented batching can introduce its own complexity. If the state of one batch is dependent on the state of another batch, shared contexts may become troublesome. The method for creating the batches is equally important. Don't calculate the number of batches then for each batch Skip and Take. You'll be introducing O(n^2). Instead, iterate once and create batches as needed.

The preferred way to scale, is to scale horizontally. We can scale horizontally inside the application by introducing multi-threading, or we can scale horizontally at the application level by adding more load-balance instances. Let's look at each.

Multi-threading

Multi-threading is awesome! I wish I could clone myself and do hundreds of tasks simultaneously. That of course would lead to issues with how to feed, shelter, and coordinate all the me's. We have the same problems when multi-threading our applications. Spinning up a bunch of threads that are not needed is wasteful. We should only spin them up when we have something to feed them. Too many threads will exhaust RAM and the house that is our computer hardware will become overcrowded. Then there is coordinating them. If each of the me's need to carry the schedule of what all the other me's are doing, managing that context would be burdensome. Managing context and state are not easy problems.

Let's take a look at how we can use multi-threading to our advantage. For this example, we will revisit our old friend the *CsvReader*. We will read a large file representing widget data. Processing the widget is somewhat intensive. So, we will multi-thread that portion of our logic. After that, we will save the results to the database.

Remember that our *CsvReader* created in an earlier chapter takes in a file path and a function for turning a line into an object of some type. Here's how we could use that CsvReader to process a file.

```
1 internal Task ProcessFile(string filePath)
2 {
3    var rdr = new CsvReader<Task>(filePath, line =>
4    {
5       var widget = new Widget(line);
6       return Task.Run(() => _widgetLogic.ProcessWidget(widget))
7       .ContinueWith(t =>
8       {
9          if (t.Exception != null)
10         {
11            throw t.Exception;
12         }
13         return _widgetProvider.Save(widget);
14      });
15   });
16
17   return Task.WhenAll(rdr.Read());
18 }
```

Ok, so there's a lot going on there. Let's break it down. Instead of having our *CsvReader* returning us a bunch of widgets, we're having it return a bunch of tasks. Those tasks can now run in parallel. Also remember that our *CsvReader* takes advantage of a *yield return*, and it doesn't do any execution until someone calls Read. When *WhenAll* on line 17 goes to inspect all the tasks, it will cause the iteration. This is where really understanding how a yield return works can pay huge dividends.

We stated that *ProcessWidget* may take some time to complete. That is why we wrapped it in a *Task.Run()*. If we hadn't, it could slow down iterating the file, because the tasks we are trying to gather would not be created until the call to *Save*. The creation of each *Task* would be delayed meaning less widgets being processed at the same time.

Using *ContinueWith* allows us to chain tasks. Be advised that exception handling looks a little different though, and the code above may not be the best way to handle an exception. The *t* on line 7 represent the *Task* returned by line 6.

That call to *WhenAll* on line 17 will race through the file and collect all the tasks coming out of the *CsvReader*. Unfortunately, this code is problematic, not because there is a lot of task manipulation, but because there is no throttling. If the file being processed is relatively small, code of this style will execute blisteringly fast. When the file gets larger, one of two problems will arise.

The first is the number of connections we're making to the database. The connection pool is limited in size. If processing happens quickly or saving takes longer because the table is large with indexes being rebuilt, we will exhaust connections to the database and the calls inside the widget provider will fail when they try to open a connection.

The other problem doesn't deal with the connection pool. It does deal with the thread pool and memory allocation. If the call to *ProcessWidget* takes too long and the file is large, we could potentially have thousands of tasks or more running. Eventually, we may exhaust the thread pool preventing new tasks from starting across the application or we could run into an *OutOfMemoryException*.

In either case, our problem is that our code is too fast! It runs faster than its dependencies allow which ultimately consumes too many system resources. Isn't that a nice problem to have? Ok, so we've potentially got two problems. How do we solve them? Well, like many things in software, there is more than one answer.

Batching

One of the above problems is the sheer number of database connections we are making. By adding a method to the widget provider that takes in a collection to save multiple widgets in one call, we can send them in a batch and reduce the number of connections required. We could implement batching in a couple of different ways.

One way would be to could create a queue in the provider. When the queue gets big enough, make the call to the database. We could also not use the continue with and implement some sort of queue between the call to process and the call to save.

I'm going to choose a different route, let's give the CsvReader some batching functionality.

```
 1  public IEnumerable<IEnumerable<T>> ReadBatched(int batchSize)
 2  {
 3      StreamReader rdr = new StreamReader(_path);
 4      if (FileHasHeader)
 5      {
 6          //ignore the first line
 7          rdr.ReadLine();
 8      }
 9      while (!rdr.EndOfStream)
10      {
11          yield return GetBatch(batchSize, rdr);
12      }
13  }
14
15  private IEnumerable<T> GetBatch(int batchSize, StreamReader rdr)
16  {
17      string line;
18      T item;
19      while (--batchSize >= 0 && (line = rdr.ReadLine()) != null)
20      {
21          item = null;
22          try
23          {
24              item = _lineParser(line.Split(','));
25          }
26          catch (Exception)
27          {
28              //log the error
29          }
30          if (item != null)
31          {
32              yield return item;
33          }
34      }
35  }
```

Excellent, we have added batching without creating a bunch of lists, arrays, or queues saving the *GarbageCollector* some work. Now, let's see how we can use it.

As stated in a previous chapter, we would need to do a better job of handling quoted values and values that contain commas.

```
1 internal Task ProccessFileBatched(string filePath)
2 {
3    var rdr = new CsvReader<Widget>(filePath,
4       line => new Widget(line));
5
6    var batchTasks =
7       from batch in rdr.ReadBatched(10)
8       select Task.Run(() =>
9       {
10         foreach (var widget in batch)
11         {
12            _widgetLogic.ProcessWidget(widget);
13         }
14         return _widgetProvider.Save(batch);
15      });
16   return Task.WhenAll(batchTasks);
17 }
```

A couple things are different from our first try. First, in the *Func* we pass to the *CsvReader*, we are having it create widgets instead of tasks. We will create the tasks out of the batches instead.

Second, we did not wrap the call to *ProcessWidget* into its own task. Maybe during our investigation and performance tuning we discovered the reason *ProcessWidget* was taking so long is that it was trying to access a shared resource and a *lock* statement was causing threads to stop and wait. After fixing that issue, the need to wrap *ProcessWidget* in its own *Task* is complexity that is no longer needed. In that case, the delays we have writing to the database are our bottleneck.

Then there is the obvious batching change. How large should we make each batch? That is going to largely depend on the specific problem at hand. Maybe instead of writing to the database, we are calling a micro-service via HTTP. In that case, depending on the size of a widget, a batch of 100 may be too large. On the other hand, because you are sending via HTTP, you have even fewer connections available than you would with a database. So maybe 100 is not small enough. Generally, smaller batches are better. Either via HTTP or to the database, the number of connections will be reduced by a factor equivalent to our batch size. Two is probably too small, but 10 may be enough. If you want to really fine tune your application, you may even decide that dynamically changing the batch size is the right way to go.

 Note:
We would will still want better exception handling on the call to WhenAll.

Batching, when done well, can be an excellent choice to help us mitigate performance and scaling issues.

Semaphore

Traditionally, a semaphore is a way of visually signaling some state, usually with two flags on movable arms, be they of a person or machine. You may see them used in train yards or at an airport. In computer science, we use them to signal when it is ok to continue or tell us to hold. They control access to a resource. In our case, that resource is available database connections. Semaphores control flow much more directly than guessing an appropriate batch size and operate a little like a limiter on an engine's carburetor. In C#, our go-to semaphore is the *SemaphoreSlim*. Here is an example of how we could process the file without batching, choosing to instead limit or throttle how fast the tasks get created.

```
1  internal Task ProcessFileWithSemaphore(string filePath)
2  {
3      SemaphoreSlim slim = new SemaphoreSlim(50, 50);
4      var rdr = new CsvReader<Task>(filePath, line => {
5          slim.Wait();
6          try
7          {
8              var widget = new Widget(line);
9              _widgetLogic.ProcessWidget(widget);
10             return _widgetProvider.Save(widget);
11         }
12         finally
13         {
14             slim.Release();
15         }
16     });
17
18     return Task.WhenAll(rdr.Read());
19 }
```

I like to name my semaphores slim because of the Jim Croce song. As you see, you want to always use a *try/finally* with your semaphore 'cause ya don't mess around with slim.

In this code, when execution gets to line 5 for the first 50 times, it will flow through without any issue. On the 51st call, it will wait until one of the threads reaches line 14 and releases a resource. Unfortunately, there is still another problem that I ran into while writing this code, and it is not obvious. The problem surrounds line 10. We are returning the task that someone else is going to wait on. That is part of the beauty of the TPL; it allows processing to continue and things only wait where they need to. So, this method is returning the *Task*, the finally block gets called and our semaphore is releasing without actually waiting for the database connections to complete their operations. Here's the code fixed.

```
1  internal Task ProcessFileWithSemaphoreFixed(string filePath)
2  {
3     SemaphoreSlim slim = new SemaphoreSlim(50, 50);
4     var rdr = new CsvReader<Task>(filePath, async line => {
5        await slim.WaitAsync();
6        try
7        {
8           var widget = new Widget(line);
9           _widgetLogic.ProcessWidget(widget);
10          await _widgetProvider.Save(widget);
11       }
12       finally
13       {
14          slim.Release();
15       }
16    });
17
18    return Task.WhenAll(rdr.Read());
19 }
```

We added the *async* keyword to line 4. Yep, lambdas can be asynchronous too. Previously, we returned the *Task* from *Save*. This time, because we are awaiting the call to *Save* on line 10, we are ensuring we are not creating too many connections to the database.

What I'd like you to think about here is visualizing the data flow through the system. In your minds eye, see the file on disk, the stream that is reading it, data flowing through the reader, getting processed and finally being saved to the database. All of that work is being done simultaneously as data streams off the disk. In both our first stab at this problem and in our batching solution, we streamed that data off disk as fast as possible into memory for continued processing. This example with the semaphore is different. We're actually throttling how fast we read the file. The reader is only doling out the data as fast as the semaphore allows. The data is on disk; it's not going anywhere. There's no need to load it all into memory faster than we can process it. We can adjust the performance by adjusting the size of the semaphore. We would ideally make that configurable. Maybe this application is running in the middle of the night, so we can use all the connections we want, or maybe we are running during business hours. In that case, database connection may be at a premium and we want to limit only 5 connections at a time.

In the end, you may find that you need to do batching because of constraints of another system and you are still running too hot so you need a semaphore too. Either way, know thy tools, and know how they can help you solve different problems.

Load Balancing and Message Queues

While looking at multi-threading, we discussed how to get the most out of our hardware. What if our problem is bigger than one file? When web sites get enough traffic, load balancing is often introduced by the network or infrastructure teams. The industry is changing though, and we must adapt with it. Micro-services are all the rage and with good reason. Monolithic web applications are difficult to maintain. As much as possible, we want to distribute the load to other applications. If we have a load balanced web site, but it funnels data to a non-load-balanced back-end service, there is really no point in load balancing the web site. In our efforts to make the code and infrastructure more maintainable, we may introduce new bottlenecks if our microservices do not also scale. If our microservice is deployed as a web application, traditional use of load balancer may be one way to solve the problem.

That's only half the story though. In a lot of industries, web applications are only one place of many where data feeds into the overall system. We may be pulling in data from any number of partners which must get processed. Those processes may be kicked off by a scheduling system like Hangfire. Should we stand up a web service so that we can load balance? That sounds like overkill. Additionally, new technologies are being developed in the cloud. Serverless functions running in containers are an ideal choice for a lot of businesses today. Why spin up hardware to run all day when we only have a need during nightly processing? How do we take in data from a single source and fan out the processing to dozens of serverless functions?

That's where message queues and event streaming services come into play. Rabbit MQ and Kafka are two popular choices today. Many cloud offerings have ways of pushing data from a variety of message queues to serverless functions. There are several appealing message queues available from the cloud offerings as well. Regardless of the event queue of choice, care must be taken to realize maximum potential.

 Many cloud offerings will try to sell you on the benefits of their services while simply ignoring viable open-source options. The do have some really nice features like enhanced logging or telemetry that integrate seamlessly with other infrastructure running in the cloud. Whether you choose an open-source solution or one of the big cloud offerings, remember: Interfaces are Illustrations of needs, not infrastructure. If your interfaces are tied to one specific technology, it may be impossible to move to a different cloud later. You may never move to another cloud, but that should be a decision for the business to make. Tying your code to one implementation takes that choice away and makes your code more susceptible to breaking changes not in your control.

Let's revisit the file processing we looked at for multi-threading.

```
1 internal Task ProccessWithMessageQueue(string filePath)
2 {
3    var rdr = new CsvReader<Task>(filePath, line =>
4      _widgetQueueProvider.Enqueue(new Widget(line))
5    );
6    return Task.WhenAll(rdr.Read());
7 }
```

Things change a lot when you change paradigms. In a way, you can say we've expanded the scope of the single responsibility principle to encompass entire applications. The only thing this application is responsible for now is validating that the information on disk is something that can be processed. All other processing, business logic, and serialization is now shunted off to a serverless function, and that function (application) is responsible for handling domain specific logic instead of having to deal with a file or some other input mechanism. It's like Onion Architecture expanded. In Onion Architecture, the domain model is at the core. Here, we've put all domain logic into a place where it can run regardless of the physical input source.

Shallot Architecture

We may have many different serverless functions or containers handling various kinds of domain models. Each container or function is of right its own application. As discussed earlier, Onion architecture is great for applications, but it may be overkill for some libraries. The reality is that as we move into the cloud our applications are getting smaller and looking more like libraries. They do have all the same needs though. They need to talk to infrastructure, keep their business logic contained, and have common ways of communicating through domain driven models. They need the whole onion.

This is where I'd like to propose a new term: Shallot Architecture.

When you look at a shallot, it looks like a misshapen onion. Start to peel it away and what you'll find is that there are several smaller cloves inside, each clove having its own core. If you cut horizontally across a shallot and look at a cross-section, you may even find that within a clove there are multiple cores. Cut vertically, and you will find that all the cores connect at the base.

If I'm going to propose a new term, I had better define it.

- Shallot architecture adheres to all the same principles as Onion Architecture including a strong reliance on dependency inversion, externalizing infrastructure, and allowing the domain logic to function independently.
- Shallot architecture is no different from Onion Architecture except that it describes more than only layers within a single application.
- Implementing Shallot Architecture means analyzing the system as a whole, rather than an individual application.
- Domain models are central. They are contracts to use for communicating not only between layers, but also between applications.
- Within the larger domain that is the system, smaller domains exist in unison.
- Maintaining Shallot architecture means recognizing that as the system scales, obstructions to a smaller domain become obstructions to the larger domain that is the system.

Too many times at numerous companies and institutions around the globe, there are situations where engineering teams become siloed. Each engineering team may be responsible for only one clove of the shallot, but those cloves must grow together. No two cloves look alike. Some will have more layers than others. A clove could be a micro-service, serverless function, or Nuget package.

If a package is developed without dependency inversion in mind, it becomes difficult for consumers of the package to unit test. The same can be said for micro-services. If there is not a common set of domain models clearly defined, as one service begins to extend one, things like identifiers can become mismatched. If each clove is using a different datastore, they each may have a different way of uniquely identifying an object. This is not to say they cannot have different data stores. In fact, with micro-services, we want them to have individual data stores. That being said, knowing how to uniquely identify an object shouldn't change between applications.

Having a common way of expressing ideas within the larger domain is critical. Those ideas are expressed in models. If the model needs logic to exist in a good state, you are tying that logic to not only other layers in the application, but potentially other applications in the system. The open/closed principle applies here as well. Objects (models) should be open for extension but closed for modification. If a property of a model is a *decimal* in one application, it should likely not be a *float* in another.

One application can be written in C# and another in Java. Regardless of language, many concepts have one-to-one mappings between languages. The idea of what a specific model is should not change or be modified. Applications can extend the idea of a model and add new properties to track things they need.

Many of the SOLID principles can be applied to applications. Whether you are talking about the single responsibility principle, the open/closed principle, or the dependency inversion principle, all of them can be thought of in terms of the way systems and applications interact.

Don't look at the whole onion. Do look at the whole shallot.

You cannot improve what you do not measure

I once heard a scientist say, "It does not exist if you cannot measure it." I found the statement to be rather profound. In software, we measure all kinds of things. Code coverage is often measured for our tests, but what do we gain from it? Code coverage is important because we know that more tests, generally, prevent more bugs. The business will likely measure how much time is spent on fixing bugs versus developing features. Feature work has more value for multiple reasons. If we spend a little more time writing tests as a part of our feature work, we spend a lot less time fixing bugs. By measuring code coverage, we get an idea of how much risk we have. If we measure coverage, we know how to improve quality and reduce risk.

Unfortunately, we may be missing out on all kinds of ways to improve because we do not measure.

Performance Tests

A lot of this book has focused on unit tests, with some emphasis on integration tests, but there are other kinds of tests. Performance tests can be a valuable strategy in your overall testing strategy, and they fall into a couple of categories.

Load Tests

Load tests will test that the system can perform under anticipated load. They can help you gather KPIs or Key Performance Indicators to ensure the system can meet SLAs or Service Level Agreements. Generally, for these kinds of tests, you want to have an environment that matches your production environment.

When you develop these tests, you should ensure they are not too narrowly focused. For example, in a web application, testing only one endpoint repeatedly is not the same as testing several endpoints concurrently. Operations that read data can interfere with operations that write data. Operations that write data can block read operations. Multiple concurrent locking operations have the potential of creating deadlocks. These kinds of errors will not show up in unit tests and will rarely appear in integration tests. Deadlocks are a good way to fail SLAs. Even if you are not running into deadlocks, there may be many things causing your system to slow.

During load tests, you should make several measurements. You should record response time and time to first byte as well as things like CPU, memory, and network usage. Once you have those measurements, you will have good indicators to where your system is most vulnerable.

Stress Tests

Stress tests are a form of load test that push the system beyond expected load to find the breaking point. These are not pass/fail tests. These are tests intended to make your system fail so that you know how, when, and where it will.

During stress tests, you should record all the same metrics as described in the load tests above. Armed with that information, you can mitigate system failures. For example, if you know the system starts to fail above a certain number of requests per minute, your infrastructure teams can create alerts based on requests per minute. When the alerts go off, you can spin up new hardware to prevent system failures. It is a lot easier and a lot less stressful to mitigate errors before they happen than to deal with the aftermath of a system failure.

As we move into the cloud, types of metrics to be captured during load and stress tests change slightly. More and more we are taking advantages of autoscaling. Perhaps the system won't fail because it scales automatically. However, it will cost more. Do we know how it scales; do we know how much it will cost?

Hopefully, we don't haven any pesky $O(n^2)$ algorithms getting in our way. If we do, scaling may become cost prohibitive. When we think about costs, we also need to think about data storage. Does it scale too? Perhaps, to build out our highly available and highly scalable infrastructure we are prepopulating caches and de-normalizing data. This can be especially costly where we have many-to-many relationships. The sheer volume of data produced could become cost prohibitive.

When stress testing the system, we should also simulate more data in the system. As your business grows, so too will the data it stores. I've seen it happen before. Systems run fine until they reach some critical tipping point, then they don't. As we move to the cloud, that sentence may be changed to "Systems are cost effective until they reach some critical tipping point, then they are not."

Logs

Chances are that every application you write has some form of logging. A successful logging strategy is critical to troubleshooting success. Logging can certainly help us measure. Unfortunately, many times logging information is not very useful. How many times have you seen an error message like "An error has occurred" or "Exception: NullReferenceException"? It is almost better to have no logging at all than logs that opaque. The best logging should be both structured and contextual.

Structured Logging

Structured logging gives us the ability to pass meaningful data to our logs. Take this fictional log message for example: "Could not retrieve book with id: 1701." If we want to find out how many times we have had trouble retrieving a book, we would have to query the logs with some sort of wildcard search, because the ID is included in the message. If we want to find out how many times we have issues with that specific book, again, we must again use a wildcard search.

Structured logging allows us to query specifics. It is more than simply a bunch of strings which need parsing. Let's look at our example of failing to retrieve a book. We would log "Could not retrieve book" and send in a data structure which includes the ID. Typically, that data structure would be a JSON payload. Then we can query for either the ID or the message without need for a wildcard search. We can also create queries with multiple parameters instead of attempting to create some complicated regular expression.

Contextual Logging

Take the previous example where there is trouble retrieving a book. When did it happen? Did it happen when the user was looking for a book to purchase or did it happen when the user was trying to make their purchase? Knowing what was going on in the system at the time the error occurred could be the clue we need to solve the riddle. Modern logging frameworks collect information throughout the stack so you can find those things out. I'd like to show you a trick. I wish I could take credit for it, but alas I cannot. It will help you a lot with your contextual logging though.

 Thus far I have tried while writing this book to not be too specific about libraries, so as to not advocate for one library over another. This example will be specific to the Microsoft.Extensions.Logging.Abstractions library. It is a fantastic way to implement logging. As of this writing, I have not found a way to gain all the benefits it provides without also pulling in a reference to Microsoft.Extensions.DepencyInjection. I dislike pulling in more references than I need. But alas, you win some and lose some. This example will not dive into all the ways the same library can be used for structured logging, of which there are several. It will focus exclusively on the contextual logging aspects it provides.

When using an *ILogger* from the *Microsoft.Extensions.Logging* namespace, you can use what it calls scope. Example:

```
1 using (_logger.BeginScope("add context here"))
2 {
3     CallAnotherMethod();
4 }
```

If inside *CallAnotherMethod* you use the logger to log something, it will include the scope from higher on the stack. That context will even carry through asynchronous calls which could be executing on different threads. Amazing! How many times have you thought about carrying information down the stack like a correlation id so that you can connect different log messages together? I have, a lot. This nearly completely solves that problem. Ok, so now that we have some good contextual logging, let's make sure to use it to handle unhandled errors. Often, right at the top of your stack, you want to have some kind of catch-all *catch* block in case you missed any exceptions. You use a catch-all to prevent your user from seeing information which they shouldn't see or may be meaningless to them.

```
 1 public void TopLevelMethod()
 2 {
 3     try
 4     {
 5         using (_logger.BeginScope("add context here"))
 6         {
 7             CallAnotherMethod();
 8         }
 9     }
10     catch (Exception ex)
11     {
12         _logger.LogError(ex, "unhandled error");
13     }
14 }
```

Unfortunately, in this case we will not capture the scope. Why? It is because when execution gets into the *catch* block, the *using* block has terminated and the scope is gone. Here's where the trick comes. The *when* clause of a *catch* block executes in the original context. So, if you are executing code in the *when* clause, the *using* statement hasn't terminated yet.

```
 1  public void TopLevelMethod2()
 2  {
 3    try
 4    {
 5      using (_logger.BeginScope("add context here"))
 6      {
 7        CallAnotherMethod();
 8      }
 9    }
10    catch (Exception ex) when (HandleException(ex, true))
11    {
12    }
13  }
14
15  private bool HandleException(Exception ex, bool propogate = false)
16  {
17    _logger.LogError(ex, "unhandled error");
18    return propogate;
19  }
```

If an exception were thrown inside *CallAnotherMethod*, this is the order in which execution would occur by line number: 6, 7, 10, 15-19, 8, 11. The beauty of this is that not only does it capture the context from line 5, but also all the context created lower in the stack inside *CallAnotherMethod* and any methods it calls. You can even change the behavior based on the type of exception. Perhaps your team has a common way of throwing exceptions based on business rules which are automatically logged. No need to log them again here, so don't. Then you can handle all other exceptions here.

Contextual logging combined with structured logging adds all sorts of ways to collect data about your system. Combined with a logging platform with robust querying capabilities, you have the makings of numerous measurements which you can use to improve your system, but that's only half the story.

Telemetry

Sometimes we look to caching to improve performance, and there are times when caching will obviously help. What if we're trying to answer the questions "Will caching help here?" or "How much is our existing cache really helping?" To answer both of those questions, we must measure cache hits and cache misses. Do users request the same items repeatedly, or do different users tend to ask for different things? The only way to find out is to measure cache hits and misses. Maybe the caching system can tell us; maybe it can't. If it can't, then

You cannot improve what you do not measure

we must actively record it for ourselves.

Sometimes we are told where there is a performance issue. The Wonder Widget page is taking too long to load. Our job is to find out why. Is it because the JavaScript is taking too long to render? Is it because our web server is overloaded? Maybe it's because the micro-service responsible for Widget data is taking too long. Maybe the widget service is sitting on the same hardware as the billing service and it is taking all the resources leaving nothing for the Widget service. In all those cases, if we haven't been measuring, we have no idea where to improve. That is where telemetry comes in.

Telemetry is more than simply logging. It is actively collecting quarriable data. When you have a heavy reliance on another service, taking the time to measure the response times of that service can be hugely beneficial to your performance tuning. Your service may be running fine all day long, but that 3rd party service gets hammered mid-afternoon. It slows down and in-turn slows down your application. By recording telemetry, you can see that kind of information.

Imagine your product owner wants to know how often a particular feature is used. The UI developers may want to record how many times certain buttons are clicked. Or maybe the business would like to find out how many times orders are canceled. What is the state of orders that get canceled? In order to know, you must actively measure it. A robust logging system may be able to answer some of those questions, but many logging systems are not built for report generation with such fine grain details or huge volumes of data.

Storing large volumes of data that nobody uses might be considered a waste. However, sometimes you don't know the questions you'll need to ask. Also, the business might not even know the kinds of questions they could ask if they had the right data available. For me personally, no system is complete without a telemetry strategy. We may not record all the things, but we should have an easy way to record them, should we want to.

Assembly Scanning

After we've developed our software, the things we deliver, aside from scripts and a few other artifacts, are assemblies. There are tools which can scan those assemblies to give us more insight into what we're delivering. They look at assemblies from an outside perspective giving us feedback on quality and security. Let's look at the many ways that assembly scanning can help us.

Security

In today's age of application development, many problems we face have already been solved. As engineers, we try not to reinvent the wheel. If our task was to build a car or piece of machinery, we wouldn't spend time designing a new wheel. Instead, we would focus on what we need out of a wheel and find one already produced that matches our expectations. Many open-source libraries function in a similar way. We don't need to design a way to do database calls or set up http endpoints. Those problems have already been solved many times over.

Unfortunately, no software is invulnerable, and from time-to-time new vulnerabilities surface. The more external dependencies we have, open-source or not, the more risk we have that is outside of our control. Take for example the Heartbleed security bug that surfaced in 2014. It was very significant and had been in place for over two years! Fortunately, all the big players worked together to minimize risk and get a fix out to the market rapidly. Few newly discovered security flaws get as much press as it.

We may have dozens of outside dependencies in our code. If such a dependency is via a purchased license, it usually comes with some level of support. When a new security vulnerability is assessed, the providing company will usually communicate to all their customers directly, informing you how to mitigate it.

The open-source world is much different. Depending on the number of open-source libraries you consume, it could easily take a full-time position to review all their documentation on a regular basis, and I've never met anyone where that is their primary responsibility. Fortunately, there is a better way.

Several tools exist that can scan your assemblies to find all the outside dependencies and compare them to published security reports. By incorporating one of these tools into our build pipeline, we can be notified the moment it is known. From there, we can assess the risk to come up with a mitigation plan.

Code Complexity

As mentioned in a previous chapter, algorithmic complexity can be spread across many layers. Nested loops may not be obvious. There are however other ways in which code can be complex and more costly.

Cyclomatic complexity is a metric we can use to mitigate additional risk. It can be described as a measure of all the potential paths our application could take. Remember our maxim that too many ifs make for iffy code. Well, cyclomatic complexity is measuring exactly that. The more paths our code can take, the harder it is to maintain and the more likely a bug will surface. I will not make an exhaustive dissertation on cyclomatic complexity here. I do however encourage you to learn more and use a tool to measure it.

Duplicate and Unused Code

Remember our maxim "The best refactors make extensive use of the delete key." Fortunately, many of these scanning tools make it easy for us to remember to use the delete key. When we take on a refactor, we may copy lines of code from one place to another. Scanning tools will identify those places where we forgot to delete the old code. Basically, they measure cruft which is one form of the dreaded technical debt. They help us keep the cruft out.

Your legacy is production code

Almost no one will admit to enjoying working in legacy code. That term comes with such a stigma as to make developers shudder with dread. The first version of this maxim was "Legacy code is any code running in production," and it's true. The moment you ship code to production it becomes legacy code. It is the legacy of you and your team. You write legacy code every day. It sounds dreadful, until you embrace it. You can't define legacy code any other way. You can say "it is using an older painful library", or it is "monolithic in nature", or it is "tightly coupled." None of those have anything to do with "legacy." To me using the term "legacy code" is equivalent to saying, "old code is bad code." It simply is not true. Well-structured code will live a long time. SOLID foundations are long lived.

When you embrace this ideology, suddenly your code changes too. You'll find yourself leaving a lot less "to-dos" in comments. Your unit test coverage will go up. You will embrace dependency inversion because you know things will change, and you don't want the pain of refactoring more than is needed. On the whole, your code will be better. Ship code worthy of your legacy.

The only permanence is a lack thereof

Have you ever worked with a developer who was, to put it politely, overly protective of their code? I have, more than once. I never want to be that guy. This is a simple reminder to me that things change. In fact, well-structured code does change over time. It adapts or is adapted. The software industry changes so we make changes. The industry your company specializes in changes, so the code changes. Being agile and resilient means being able to adapt to change. There have been times in my career where I built something I was exceptionally proud of; then only a year later I had to delete it all. It happens.

Similar to how using a *for* loop for a wait statement on a Commodore 64 seems absurd by today's standards, some of the things in this book may become outdated. Hopefully not too soon, but it will happen, and I'm ok with that.

What's not on the list?

In the preface of this book, I described my list of maxims as being a list of general truths that have helped me in my career. The list has changed over time. Usually, when an item is added it comes from my "ideas under review". There are a few more items under review which have not made the list yet. They are however worthy of discussion, and this book would not feel complete without them. The remainder of this book is about those items.

Why haven't they made the list yet? To answer that, it is worth looking at what qualified an item to make the list. Items are added as under review first. Usually, they are large in scope and the essences of their meanings are not yet distilled. As time goes on and more thought given, I find ways to shorten them. Like a chef reducing a stock, I boil them down to their most critical components. After being refined and trimmed, if given more time they still feel right, I add them to the list. So, if it hasn't made the list yet, but it is in this book, it simply means I haven't found a pithy way of expressing it. It hasn't become a maxim.

Reflection do's and don'ts

I must begin the conversation about reflection cautioning you to try not to use it. In a previous chapter I stated that generics was one of the best features added to C#. The features related to generics in C# and .NET are robust and among the best in modern languages. When it comes to dynamically changing your application behavior based on types, you can do a lot with generics. So, try to reach for generics first. All that being said, there are times that generics won't get you what you need, and reflection can be a very useful tool.

Because C# is strongly typed, there are a lot of things we can do to inspect objects at runtime. That inspection of an object and its type is done through reflection. With reflection, you can build incredibly powerful algorithms. Do not be fooled though. Reflection is scary. Maybe that is my pithy statement about reflection. Reflection is scary and potentially downright dangerous. When done improperly, it changes C# into a language without type safety. Ironic, the reason you can do reflection is its type safety, but using it potentially means throwing away the type safety.

Another of the items under review is "Reflection is ok at startup, not runtime." Unfortunately, that statement is not entirely accurate and is a bit too specific. Startup is technically runtime. It would be more accurate to say that if you have a need to do reflection, you should only do it once. Not only is reflection scary; it can be expensive too.

Not all reflection calls are expensive though. Some are quite cheap. This does not make things any clearer. The waters we are wading into are quite muddy, and the danger could be lurking anywhere. When tracking down a bug and I encounter reflection, that is exactly how I feel. What have I wandered into? If you must use reflection, use comments! Let those following you know where the path is and where not to stray.

Ok, so reflection is dangerous, scary, and expensive. Why use it? Well, sometimes, it is the right tool. IOC containers use it heavily. That is why we can rely on dependency injection so heavily. They inspect constructors. Test frameworks use it both for executing tests and for mocking objects. Test attributes, like all attributes, don't do anything by themselves. Some other class must use reflection to inspect the attributes to determine appropriate behavior. Attributes are commonly used for Authorization in MVC logging, and object notation for serialization. In this chapter I am not going to show a full example how to create any of the above. Taking on a full example of any one of them and doing it well is beyond the scope of this book. Each could be a treatise or book of its own. Instead, I will focus on the reflection itself.

It takes skill, but it is possible to use reflection that is not dangerous for the consumer and is not expensive. Before we dive into the specifics, let's lay some ground rules.

- Inspecting a type is not expensive.
- Invoking what you have inspected is expensive.
- Do not rely on pattern or naming convention to find type members.
- When dealing with expensive reflection calls, try to execute them only once.
- Avoid exposing any objects from the *System.Reflection* namespace in any of your interfaces.

 Note:
The *Type* and *Attribute* types are in the *System* namespace.

Now that the ground rules have been laid, let's get down to specifics. First, let's talk about the stuff that is not expensive ok to do at any time. The following method doesn't do anything. It is simply a collection of examples.

```
1  void OkReflectionExamples<T>(MyType someObject)
2  {
3      // getting a referene to a Type
4      Type t = typeof(T);
5      t = someObject.GetType();
6
7      // getting member information
8      PropertyInfo propInfo = t.GetProperty(nameof(MyType.MyProperty)
9          , BindingFlags.Public | BindingFlags.Instance);
10
11     MethodInfo methodInfo = t.GetMethod(
12         nameof(MyType.MyMethod), BindingFlags.DeclaredOnly);
13
14     //dicovering attributes
15     var attribute = t.GetCustomAttribute<MyAttribute>();
16
17     //discovering if a type is derived from or implements another
18     bool inherits = typeof(object).IsAssignableFrom(t);
19  }
```

Inspecting information about a type is generally not expensive. Most of the operations above operate in O(1) time. Reflection methods that do filtering such as *GetProperty* and *GetMethod* may do a little more work, but generally operate quickly.

Now, let's look at more expensive, and potentially unsafe operations.

```
1 void ExpensiveReflectionExamples(object someObject,
2   PropertyInfo someProperty, MethodInfo someMethod)
3 {
4   someProperty.GetValue(someObject);
5   someMethod.Invoke(someObject, null);
6 }
```

These are both dangerous examples. On lines 4 and 5, we are invoking members of a type without a reference to the type itself. This demonstrates how reflection ignores type safety. They are attempting to invoke members of the class that may or may not exist. If *someObject* did not have *someProperty* or *someMethod* those lines would throw an exception. Even if we were sure that the method or property did exist on *someObject*, both of those calls are expensive compared to execution via a type safe reference. There are ways to build methods via reflection that are not expensive. In the next example we will build such a method.

For this example, we will return to our old friend the CSV, but instead of reading a CSV, we will be generating one. We would like a method that can take in a collection of any model. It will produce a header row with the property names. Each of the rest of the lines in the CSV will represent one item in the collection with the values of each property. If a property throws and exception, we want to display "error". If a property is null, we want to display "null". First, we will create an interface, because we want all consumers to be able to unit test their code.

```
1 public interface ICsvGenerator
2 {
3   IEnumerable<string> OutputToCsv<T>(
4     IEnumerable<T> collection, char delimiter = ',');
5 }
```

Each string in the output *IEnumerable* will represent one line. It will be up to the consumer to take each line and either write it to disk or stream it to their consumer. By returning an *IEnumerable* and using a *yield return,* we can generate a CSV of any size. Otherwise, if the collection was large, getting the contents of the entire CSV may bloat our memory. Here is a naïve implementation.

```
1  public class CsvGeneratorSlow : ICsvGenerator
2  {
3      public IEnumerable<string> OutputToCsv<T>(
4          IEnumerable<T> collection, char delimiter = ',')
5      {
6          var properties = typeof(T).GetProperties(
7              BindingFlags.Public | BindingFlags.Instance)
8              .Where(p => p.CanRead).ToArray();
9
10         //this line returns the header row
11         yield return properties.Select(p => EscapeAndWrap(p.Name))
12             .Aggregate((p1, p2) => $"{p1}{delimiter}{p2}");
13
14         foreach (var item in collection)
15         {
16             yield return
17                 properties.Select(p => EscapeAndWrap(GetValue(p, item)))
18                 .Aggregate((p1, p2) => $"{p1}{delimiter}{p2}");
19         }
20     }
21     private string GetValue<T>(PropertyInfo prop, T obj)
22     {
23         //this method is private,
24         // the type safety of T is constrained by generics
25         // the type safety of prop was checked in OutputToCsv
26         try
27         {
28             var val = prop.GetValue(obj);
29             return val == null ? "null" : val.ToString();
30         }
31         catch (Exception)
32         {
33             return "error";
34         }
35     }
36     private static string EscapeAndWrap(string input)
37     {
38         return $"\"{input.Replace("\"", "\"\"")}\"";
39     }
40 }
```

The *EscapeAndWrap* method will wrap values in quotes and escape quotes in the value.

We are doing a fair amount of error handling and prevention. On line 6 we ensure that we only retrieve public properties that we can read (they have a getter). We call the *ToArray* method because we know we will be reading that collection a lot and we don't want to continue to run that logic when once will suffice. We are also taking advantage of the *yield return* to ensure we don't blow out the memory of any consumer. When getting the value for any given property, we are protecting ourselves and the consumer from any exception that may occur in a getter.

The problem resides on line 28. It is dynamically getting the property value for every property on every object. To speed things up, we should have a compiled statement ready to execute. That means we must do a bunch of work up front in order to speed this up overall. Remember, we want to try to do expensive operations only once, not the hundreds or thousands of times that would be done with this implementation.

Before we show the whole example, let's look at how we can use expression trees to compile getting the value of a property. The *_toString* variable is a reference to *object.ToString()*.

```
1  private static Func<T, string> BuildPropertyGetter(PropertyInfo prop)
2  {
3      // we're going to build an expression
4      // if the property is a value type
5      //   item => item.Property.ToString()
6      // otherwise
7      //   item => item.Property == null ? "null" : item.Property.ToString();
8      var type = typeof(T);
9      var input = Expression.Parameter(typeof(T), "item");
10
11     var propExpression = Expression.Property(input, prop);
12
13     var toString = prop.PropertyType != typeof(string)
14         ? (Expression)Expression.Call(propExpression, _toString)
15         : propExpression;
16
17     if (prop.PropertyType.IsValueType)
18     {
19         var lambda = Expression.Lambda<Func<T, string>>(toString, input)
20             .Compile();
21         return item => EscapeAndWrap(lambda(item));
22     }
23     else
24     {
25         var nullExpression = Expression.Constant(null);
26         var isNull = Expression.Equal(propExpression, nullExpression);
27         var condition = Expression.Condition(isNull,
28             Expression.Constant("null"), toString);
29
30         var lambda = Expression.Lambda<Func<T, string>>(condition, input)
31             .Compile();
32         return item => EscapeAndWrap(lambda(item));
33     }
34 }
```

The *T* parameter is coming from a *static* class which I will show momentarily. The comment at the top explains what is happening. Essentially, when you look at *item.Property.ToString()*, all the parts of that line must be assembled. The same is true for the ternary operation. This method returns a *Func* which takes in an object of type T and returns the value of a single property wrapped in quotes for use in the CSV. One of the key things to see here are on lines

19 and 20. The *Compile* method creates strongly typed references to the properties as if you had typed them directly.

Below is the entire implementation.

```
1  public class CsvGeneratorFast : ICsvGenerator
2  {
3    static MethodInfo _toString;
4    static MethodInfo _aggregate;
5
6    static CsvGeneratorFast()
7    {
8      _toString = typeof(object).GetMethod("ToString");
9      _aggregate = typeof(Enumerable).GetMethods()
10       .First(m =>
11       m.Name == nameof(Enumerable.Aggregate) &&
12       m.GetGenericArguments().Length == 1)
13       .MakeGenericMethod(typeof(string));
14   }
15
16   public IEnumerable<string> OutputToCsv<T>(
17     IEnumerable<T> objects, char delimiter = ',')
18   {
19     return CsvBuilder<T>.Actual(objects, delimiter);
20   }
21
22   private delegate string LineBuilder<T>(char delimiter, T item);
23   private delegate string HeaderBuilder(char delimiter);
24
25   private static class CsvBuilder<T>
26   {
27     static LineBuilder<T> _lineBuilder;
28     static HeaderBuilder _headerBuilder = null;
29
30     static CsvBuilder()
31     {
32       var properties = typeof(T).GetProperties(
33         BindingFlags.Public | BindingFlags.Instance)
34         .Where(p => p.CanRead).ToArray();
35
```

```
36      if (properties.Count == 0)
37      {
38        return;
39      }
40
41      _headerBuilder = delimiter =>
42        properties.Select(p => EscapeAndWrap(p.Name))
43        .Aggregate((s1, s2) => $"{s1}{delimiter}{s2}");
44
45      var valueGetters = properties.Select(prop =>
46        BuildPropertyGetter(prop)).ToArray();
47
48      _lineBuilder = (delimiter, item) =>
49        valueGetters.Select(getter =>
50        {
51          try
52          {
53            return getter(item);
54          }
55          catch (Exception)
56          {
57            return "error";
58          }
59        })
60        .Aggregate((s1, s2) => $"{s1}{delimiter}{s2}");
61    }
62
63    public static IEnumerable<string> Actual(
64      IEnumerable<T> items, char delimiter)
65    {
66      if (items == null)
67      {
68        throw new ArgumentNullException(nameof(items));
69      }
70      if (_headerBuilder == null)
71      {
72        throw new Exception("object has no readable properties");
73      }
74      yield return _headerBuilder(delimiter);
75      foreach (var item in items)
```

```
76        {
77            yield return _lineBuilder(delimiter, item);
78        }
79    }
80
81    private static Func<T, string> BuildPropertyGetter(PropertyInfo prop)
82    {
83        // we're going to build an expression
84        // if the property is a value type
85        //   item => item.Property.ToString()
86        // otherwise
87        //   item => item.Property == null ?
88        //     "null" : item.Property.ToString();
89        var type = typeof(T);
90        var input = Expression.Parameter(typeof(T), "item");
91
92        var propExpression = Expression.Property(input, prop);
93
94        var toString = prop.PropertyType != typeof(string)
95            ? (Expression)Expression.Call(propExpression, _toString)
96            : propExpression;
97
98
99        if (prop.PropertyType.IsValueType)
100        {
101            var lambda = Expression.Lambda<Func<T, string>>
102                    (toString, input).Compile();
103            return item => EscapeAndWrap(lambda(item));
104        }
105        else
106        {
107            var nullExpression = Expression.Constant(null);
108            var isNull = Expression.Equal(propExpression, nullExpression);
109            var condition = Expression.Condition(isNull,
110                Expression.Constant("null"), toString);
111
112            var lambda = Expression.Lambda<Func<T, string>>
113                    (condition, input).Compile();
114            return item => EscapeAndWrap(lambda(item));
115        }
```

```
116        }
117
118        private static string EscapeAndWrap(string input)
119        {
120            return $"\"{input.Replace("\"", "\"\"")}\"";
121        }
122    }
123 }
```

In a previous chapter, I stated that *static* is almost as bad as *new*. In this implementation, we have used a static class, but obscured it from the consumer. This makes code for the consumer unit testable. Line 30 is where some of the magic happens. It is the type initializer; some may call it the static constructor. You have no guarantees when it will run, but it is guaranteed to run exactly once prior to the class being used. Remember, we want to do expensive operations only once, and the type initializer will only run once. Also, because the class is generic it will run once for every type of generic parameter passed in. When using a type initializer, you **must** take extra care to **never** throw an exception in it. Make sure you have handled every null reference possible, and that no exceptions will ever be thrown. In the type initializer, we created methods for getting a header and turning each model into a line. Later, when someone calls the *OutputToCsv* method, they are reused as many times as they are needed.

On lines 22 and 23, I created delegates for use in the *CsvBuilder* class. Normally I use *Action* or *Func*, but in this case, because multiple parameters are being passed in, I wanted it clearer what each parameter does.

In my tests of this relatively simple example where only one reflection call was being adapted, I saw a performance increase of 20-25% between the slow and fast versions. If more reflection calls were adapted the performance increase would be more significant. When I removed the work done by *EscapeAndWrap* the performance increase was even more noticeable.

As you can see, even in this relatively simple example, making reflection run efficiently is complicated. Reflection is indeed something to be approached with caution and a good amount of coffee.

Code Reviews

A lot of this book has been about ensuring quality. We talked about tests and how important they are to shipping quality code. We talked about SOLID principles and how they enable you to write code which is easy to maintain. Code reviews are possibly the best, best-practice you have to ensuring quality, but they are so much more than only that.

What are code reviews? Simply, they are when one or more developers review what another developer has written and give feedback. The feedback is then taken and used to improve the code before it ships. In my first job in the industry, they were done in person. One developer would pair with the author, and they would go through all the changes in the feature branch before it was merged into the trunk. It was a fantastic experience. Because they were done in person, it was much more of a conversation than how code reviews look and feel in most shops today where a tool is used to review the changes and comments are added via a web interface.

To me, the key to a good code review is conversation. Much of how I've written this book is a conversation between you the reader and me the author. I have endeavored to see things from your point of view and ask questions you may be asking. That's the second key to a good code review; ask questions. When I'm giving a code review, sometimes I know that something shouldn't be done the way it has been done. Instead of demanding that it gets fixed, I ask a question, "What happens when this variable is null?" In attempting to answer the question, the reviewee is presented with the problem and eight times out of ten, they come up with a better solution. In the other two out of ten times, something magical happens. One of two things will happen. In the first, they, the reviewee does not know and asks another question. They get an answer and learn something. In the second, they either ask another question about the code or point out something I did not see. I then learn something. This may seem counterintuitive, but I love it when I'm wrong. I take a special pleasure when I'm wrong in figuring out why I was wrong to make sure I learn something new. In the words of Adam Savage, "Failure is always an option." When we fail, it is an opportunity not presented when we succeed.

Software is an industry that changes rapidly. The only way to keep up is to keep learning. This is why code reviews are so important to me. They are built into our process to ensure quality, but they also serve to help us learn.

Today's code reviews are not usually done in person. The tools built into our source control systems for commenting and reviewing can feel very impersonal. I'm often asked to do a code review for another team. If I have not worked with the person who wrote the code, it can be difficult for me to convey that my comments are not demands, but rather the opening of a conversation. When I've had those difficulties, I'll often reach out on another channel to open the conversation more. If one tool doesn't do what you need, use another. Maybe this is my pithy maxim about code reviews: Code reviews are conversations.

Partnership

If there is one chapter I debated not including in this book, it would be this one. I call myself a full-stack generalist and a .NET specialist. I would consider myself to have an expert level of understanding in C#. I am certainly no expert in the subject of human relations. So much of what we do as software engineers, however, involves working with other people. For all the roles I interact with, I'm constantly asking myself "How I can partner with them?" I do believe that together we achieve greatness.

In the last chapter, I spoke about working with fellow engineers, but there are so many others that are a part of our success. We partner with engineers, QA personnel, and SDET's to ensure quality. We partner with development managers and architects to ensure we have a shared vision. If we have not fostered those relationships, our day-in-day-out duties can be difficult to fulfill. Partnering with them is key to a successful implementation.

It's not often, but when I do get to work with UI designers, I thoroughly enjoy it. Generally, I try to stay as far away from UI as I can. I don't know how to make things pretty. I do know how to make them function efficiently, but design is certainly not my strong suit. When developing a new feature and the opportunity does arise for me to work with a designer, I relish the opportunity to partner with them. I will almost certainly learn something. I remember one time when a UI design called for a button in a certain location. As I was working through the problem and realized that the enabling of the button depended on a drop-down having a certain value, I also realized that the existence of the button could be removed by changing the options in the drop-down. We partnered together and the UI designer agreed with me. She was so happy because it was something she had been struggling with too. Through partnership, we built a better product. I remember another time early in my career when the designer presented a form that represented a user. At the top was the user's name. In this case it said "John Doe". I pointed out that not all users only have seven characters in their name. That designer started using John Jacob Jingleheimer Schmidt in all their designs. Again, partnership made a better product.

While on the subject of UI, it would be remiss of me to not discuss UX. If you are reading this book and in the position of staffing your company, please hire a UX engineer. UI is User Interface. It is what things look like. UX is user experience. It is about the experience a user has when working with a product. If there was one place most companies fail, it is understanding the importance of focusing on UX. Experience is key for a user. It drives me crazy when I'm working with an application and I constantly have to reach for the mouse to select the text box that should have been selected when I clicked the plus sign to add an item so some collection. Extra clicks take time and are annoying, and "annoying" is not the word you want someone to describe your beautiful UI with. This may be a bit of a first world problem, but if you want to see examples of great UI and horrible UX, all you have to do is go to your TV and use a few different streaming applications. I remember one particular steaming application where the simple act of pressing up and down on the remote a few times ended up navigating to 4 different screens. Talk about confusing! So, if you are a stake holder, please hire and <u>partner</u> with a UX engineer. I'll get off my soapbox now.

Technical writers provide an extension to UI and UX. We as engineers often deal with complex and hard to understand object relations. It is critical for us to communicate effectively to the technical writing staff so they can effectively communicate to the customer. If no one understands how to use the product we are building, what use is our product. Take time to partner with the technical writers.

Product Owners, Project Managers, and Scrum leaders are all key people to partner with. They are some of my biggest allies. While PM's shouldn't contribute to sizing or pointing stories, they should absolutely be a part of the conversation. Whether you call them grooming or refinement sessions those conversations are opportunities to partner with the business. When they understand where additional difficulty lies, it is easier for them to get us the resources we need.

Lastly, and certainly not least, are customers. As engineers, we may not get many opportunities to partner with the customer, your product owner certainly does. The business definitely wants the customer to perceive the relationship as a partnership. Managing those relationships can be difficult. As I said at the top of the chapter, I am no expert on relationships. I rely heavily on my allies to navigate partnering with the customer. Our internal partnership helps promote external partnership.

So, while partnership may have nothing to do with code, it certainly deals with shipping quality resilient code.

Exit Code 0

Now that we have reached the end, my hope is that these maxims will lead you to more success. I hope that you will write more code worthy of the moniker "legacy", and that you write less cruft. I hope that you will be more resilient when faced with the challenges of both yesterday's code and tomorrow's.

If I had to sum up the maxims in a few short sentences, this is what I might say.

- When applications are built with SOLID foundations, they are more resilient. They adapt with time and the change that comes with it.
- With a broader toolset, you become more resilient.
- Quality, meaningful tests help you ship less bugs and spend more time writing features.
- Code that is easier to maintain, has greater long-term value.
- When scale goes into design, so does performance.

When I struggle with analysis paralysis, I reach for the maxims. They have often been inspirational to me. When faced with two equally complex and difficult choices to solve a particular problem, the maxims have been equally as helpful. In a way, they have become one more tool in my toolbelt.

So, go forth brave engineers with tools in hand. Cultivate many shallots. Build boldly, with scale and maintainability. May you and your code live long and prosper.

References

Autofac

A feature rich IOC container
https://autofac.org/

Git Extensions

An open source GUI for working with Git
https://gitextensions.github.io/

Expresso

A tool for working with Regex (highly recommended by me)
http://www.ultrapico.com/Expresso.htm

Hangfire

An easy way to perform background processing with scheduling.
https://www.hangfire.io/

Kafka

A distributed event streaming platform.
https://kafka.apache.org/

Microsoft.Extensions.DependencyInjection

A popular IOC container
https://www.nuget.org/packages/Microsoft.Extensions.DependencyInjection/

Microsoft.Extensions.Logging.Abstractions

A logging framework for contextual and structured logging
https://www.nuget.org/packages/Microsoft.Extensions.Logging.Abstractions/

Moq

A mocking framework for unit tests (my personal favorite)
https://github.com/moq/moq4

NSubstitute

A mocking framework for unit tests
https://nsubstitute.github.io/

NUnit

A test framework originally based on JUnit
https://nunit.org/

Onion Architecture

A collection of best practices forming an architecture strategy coined by Jeffrey Palermo.
https://jeffreypalermo.com/2008/07/the-onion-architecture-part-1/

posh-git

A powershell module with git integration
https://dahlbyk.github.io/posh-git/

Rabbit MQ

A commonly used mature message queue system
https://www.rabbitmq.com/

Selenium

A browser automation framework often used for end-to-end integration testing
https://www.selenium.dev/

Simple Injector

An incredibly fast IOC container built with SOLID in mind
https://simpleinjector.org/index.html

Unity

A 2D, 3D, VR, and AR engine
https://unity.com/

xUnit

A modern test framework written by the creators of NUnit V2 (my personal favorite)
https://xunit.net/

Index

A

abstract class   10

algorithmic complexity   37, 113, 131

assembly scanning   130

async/await   50, 120

B

batching   116

Big-O   37

C

catch   95

code coverage   61, 69, 125

code review   149

comment   111, 133, 139

component test   60

connection pool   116

contextual logging   127

cruft   109, 132

D

dependency injection   15, 64, 66

dependency inversion principle   5, 15, 124

DI. See dependency injection

E

end-to-end test   59

exception   95, 148

F

fluent interface   105

G

garbage collector   73

I

IDE. See integrated development environment

IEnumerable   21, 32, 37, 46, 141

integrated development environment   45

integration test   59

interface   13, 19, 64, 83

interface segregation principle   5, 13, 103

inversion of control   11, 15, 75, 101

IOC   47, 83, 139. See also inversion of control

L

Linq   32, 40, 105

Liskov substitution principle   5, 10

load test   125

logging   126

M

manual test   59

message queue   121

mocking   64

N

new   73

N-tier   81, 87

O

Occam's Razor   79

onion architecture   82, 87, 101, 122

open/closed principle   5, 8, 124

ORM   102

R

reflection   77, 139

regex. See regular expressions

regular expressions   45, 46

S

semaphore   119

shallot   84, 122

single responsibility principle   5, 93, 103, 106, 124

singleton   75

SOLID   5, 124, 133

static   75, 106, 148

stress test   126

structured logging   127

T

telemetry   69, 129

temporal coupling   11

testing triangle   57

thread   50, 114

thread safety   11

throw   95, 99

type initializer   148

U

unit test   60, 65, 67, 83, 86, 101

Y

yield return   21, 32, 141